"If you want a deeper under[...]
you can't do better than th[...]
apologetic attention to hist[...]
truth: land grabbing is not j[...]
of 90s-style, triumphal neoli[...]
but what we fight."
—Naomi Klein (author, *The Shock Doctrine*) and Avi Lewis (director,
   The Take)

"Tanya Kerssen's book on Honduras provides a concise and impassioned
analysis of the most acute agrarian crisis in Central America in the past
fifteen years. *Grabbing Power* exposes the linkages between a corrupt and
authoritarian political regime, an undemocratic agricultural and food
system, the criminalization of subsistence activities and social movements and deeply troubling processes of environmental destruction."
—Marc Edelman, Hunter College and the Graduate Center, City
   University of New York

"Grabbing Power represents a timely and inspiring challenge to the swell-
ing 'land grab' literature. Tanya Kerssen situates the current land grab
in Honduras as more than a momentary putsch— rather a power play
against a land and democracy movement generated by previous neoliberal land grabs in the 1990s. The story is one thing, and it is powerful; the
challenge is another, namely, that land grab analyses need to take account
of the full range and genealogy of political forces at work."
—Philip McMichael, Cornell University

"Grabbing Power by Tanya Kerssen is a small book on a huge topic: contemporary global land grabbing, in the specific context of Honduras. It
challenges many aspects of the conventional understanding of this trend,
and provokes critical thinking on what is to be done."
—Jun Borras, International Institute of Social Studies (ISS), The Hague

"This comprehensive and incisive work uncovers the power dynamics
and history of the war over land in Honduras, shedding light on the root
causes of the conflict, and the vision of the social movements fighting
not just for land and dignity, but for a radical transformation of society."
—Benjamin Dangl, author, *Dancing with Dynamite: Social Movements and
   States in Latin America*

"With this chilling description of the impacts in Honduras of the new
scramble towards land and resources, Tanya Kerssen gives faces, and voices,
to what is all too often described through statistics and trends — an ano-
nymization that is also a silencing. This is required reading for those who
wish to understand land grabbing from the point of view of the victims."
—Olivier De Schutter, United Nations Special Rapporteur on the
   Right to Food

LAND & SOVEREIGNTY SERIES

GRABBING POWER

The New Struggles for Land, Food and Democracy
in Northern Honduras

Tanya M. Kerssen

FOODFIRST
B O O K S

Oakland, CA

Food First Books
Institute for Food and Development Policy
398 60th Street, Oakland, CA 94618-1212 USA
Tel (510) 654-4400   Fax (510) 654-4551
www.foodfirst.org   foodfirst@foodfirst.org

Cover and text design by Design Action Collective
Copy editor: William Wroblewski
Proofreader: Emily Johnson

Library of Congress Cataloging-in-Publication Data

Kerssen, Tanya M.
Grabbing power : the new struggles for land, food and democracy in
northern Honduras / by Tanya M. Kerssen. – 1st ed.
    p. cm. – (Land & sovereignty series ; No. 1.)
  Includes bibliographical references and index.
  ISBN 978-0-935028-43-0 — ISBN 978-0-935028-44-7 (ebook)
  1. Peasants—Political activity—Honduras—Aguán River Valley.
  2. Agriculture—Economic aspects—Honduras—Aguán River Valley.
  3. Land use, Rural—Honduras—Aguán River Valley. 4. Aguán
  River Valley (Honduras)—Rural conditions. 5. Aguán River Valley
  (Honduras)—Economic conditions. I. Title. II. Series: Land &
  sovereignty series ; 1.
    HD1531.H6K47 2013
    338.1097283'1—dc23   2012043577

Food First Books are distributed by:
Perseus Distribution
250 West 57th Street
New York, NY 10107
Tel (212) 340-8100
www.perseusdistribution.com

Printed in Canada.
5 4 3 2 1

ACKNOWLEDGEMENTS

I wish to thank Rights Action, Alliance for Global Justice (AFGJ) and the Honduras Solidarity Network for their important work supporting grassroots movements and informing the public about the impacts of US and Canadian foreign policy in Honduras. I owe special thanks to Karen Spring and Jesse Freeston for sharing with me their nuanced understandings of the Aguán region. They both provided invaluable review of this manuscript, as did Alberto Alonso-Fradejas, Zoe Brent, Marc Edelman, Eric Holt-Giménez, Andrés León, Adrienne Pine, Annie Shattuck and William Wroblewski—none of whom bear responsibility for its final contents. Thanks also to Tyler Shipley and Ilana Nevins for their contributions; Chuck Kaufman and Raúl Mendoza for their work and solidarity; Diane and Dennis Kerssen for their immeasurable support; Martha Katigbak-Fernandez for her publishing help; Emily Johnson for proofreading; Design Action Collective for layout and design; and Roger Harris and Gerardo Torres for opening my eyes to the magnitude and significance of the Honduran resistance movement. Thank you Jesse Freeston, Roger Harris, Greg McCain and Aryeh Shell for contributing photos. Most of all, I am humbled and inspired by the peasants of Aguán who generously shared their time, testimonies and analysis (the names of most individuals have been changed or omitted for their protection). This book is dedicated to their struggle for land and dignity, and to the promise of a (food) sovereign and genuinely democratic Honduras.

CONTENTS

FOREWORD

by Eric Holt-Giménez

Land grabs are a means to power and control. This simple fact—often lost in the current debates over "large-scale land acquisitions"—is the central thesis of this book about the heroic struggle by peasants in the Aguán Valley of Honduras to keep their land in the face of the rapacious national elites bent on taking it.

"Power," wrote Frederick Douglass, "concedes nothing without a demand." Comprehending how power constructs itself globally and locally; how it avails itself of ideology, the state, the market, the army and paramilitary violence; and how it goes about violating basic human rights in order to amass wealth (and more power to protect its wealth) is essential for understanding both what drives current land grabs and what can be done to stop them.

The case of the corporate expansion of palm oil in the Aguán Valley provides these lessons within the context of late capitalism's rush on the world's natural resources. The violent recourse to "accumulation by dispossession" behind today's land grabs in Honduras goes beyond popular media accounts of land deals by foreign investors. The land being grabbed in the Aguán is being taken piece by piece as part of a long-standing class project of Honduran elites. What Honduran land grabs do have in common with global media accounts is the plantation mechanism—oil palm—and the complicity of Northern governments and multilateral development institutions. What distinguishes Honduran land grabs is the extent of the bloody violence by Honduran elites and the determined, militant resistance on the part of the peasant movements in the Aguán.

The Aguán Valley is emblematic. Land grabs here respond to both historical inequities in the Americas and to the new crises of accumulation by transnational capital, of which Latin American elites are also a part. It is also a reflection of the larger, global struggle being carried out by peasant and indigenous communities around the world. In the face of the relentless destruction of their lands and livelihoods, the peasants of the Aguán refuse to disappear.

Much has been written about food sovereignty—the right of all peoples to determine their own food and production systems. In this book, Tanya Kerssen provides a trenchant and uncompromising picture of the struggle for *land* sovereignty—people's right to live and thrive on the land that feeds them. The lessons shared in this book help us understand a world in which local peasant resistance increasingly characterizes global strategies for survival.

Eric Holt-Giménez is Executive Director of Food First/ Institute for Food and Development Policy. He is the author of *Campesino a Campesino: Voices from Latin America's Farmer to Farmer Movement for Sustainable Agriculture*, which chronicles two and a half decades of farmers' movements in Mexico and Central America.

No somos peces para vivir del agua, ni aves para vivir del aire; somos hombres y mujeres para vivir de la tierra.

We are not fish that live in the water, or birds that live in the air; we are men and women who live from the land.

—Slogan of the Unified Movement of Aguán Peasants (MUCA)

INTRODUCTION

Journalist Manuel Torres Calderón (2002) calls Honduras the "unknown country," the least known and the least understood country in Central America—primarily thought of as a "banana republic" and a US base for counter-insurgency in the 1980s. Indeed, compared to most Latin American countries, there are few English-language books about Honduras written for a popular audience. Even after the June 2009 coup that ousted president Manuel Zelaya and the massive popular movement that followed, Honduras languished in mainstream media obscurity, overshadowed by celebratory coverage of the Arab Spring. When the media did report on Honduras (or Central America in general) it generally portrayed the region as a hopeless "basket case" beset by gangs, crime and a tragically unwinnable War on Drugs. These portrayals tell us little about the structural (political and economic) causes of poverty and violence. Nor do they show us how fiercely Hondurans are fighting to take back control of their local economies, protect their families from violence, and build democracy from the ground up.

While Honduran cities are growing rapidly, marked by highly precarious working and living conditions, the majority (74 percent) of the poor are *rural*: they are peasants (*campesinos*), landless workers, indigenous and Afro-indigenous peoples (USAID 2011b, 4). As throughout Latin America, both rural and urban poverty are closely linked to the unequal distribution of

ɔrmous landholdings (known as *latifundios*) on one
holdings (*minifundios*) on the other. In Honduras,
70 percent of the farmers hold 10 percent of the
ɪdios while 1 percent of the farmers hold 25 percent of the land in massive estates (ibid.).

Over the last three decades, the poverty generated by Honduras' unequal land distribution has been magnified by climate change and natural disasters, rising food prices and land grabs for corporate agribusiness and tourism development. While deepening both urban and rural vulnerability, these events also sparked new forms of grassroots organizing and political consciousness. This book explores the dramatic expansion of agro-industrial development in northern Honduras in the neoliberal era, its relationship to strengthening elite power and the seeds of popular resistance it has paradoxically sown. Honduras is not a hopeless basket case. It is, like many countries in the Global South, a place where hunger, poverty and violence are rooted in a lack of genuine democracy (and not, as some would have it, a lack of foreign aid or economic growth). And that is precisely what Honduran peasant movements are fighting for: the democratization of land, food and political power.

Situating Honduras in the Global Land Grab

In the wake of the 2007-2008 global food, fuel and financial crises, observers have called attention to a growing trend in large-scale farmland investments, particularly in poor countries of the Global South. While reliable figures are hard to come by, estimates range from around 56.6 million to 227 million hectares of grabbed land globally (Cotula 2012). These land grabs erode local control, often re-orienting production from meeting local needs to meeting global market demands for food, feed and fuel. The impact on land-based livelihoods—those of peasants and indigenous peoples whose survival hinges directly on access to land and nature—has been deeply devastating. The term "land grab" has now become a media buzzword, a catchall phrase for the new global wave of peasant dispossession. Numerous scholars, activists and organizations[1] have been analyzing the phenomenon to understand the forces behind it, while also working to stop it (or curb its impacts) through campaigns and solidarity efforts.

New players have been identified (e.g. financial companies, pension funds, sovereign wealth funds) as the buyers of huge tracts of land. Compared to previous instances of land grabbing by colonial powers or agribusiness firms, these investors tend to be much more interested in the financial value of land (and of the resources on, under or near it) than the value of its production. Pension funds, for instance—which have quickly become one of the largest institutional investors in land—"see long-term pay-offs from the rising value of farmland and the cash flow that will in the meantime come from crop sales, dairy herds or meat production" (GRAIN 2011a). The speculative nature of land acquisitions by a new set of global actors—in the context of the food, fuel and financial crisis—is a defining feature of the new land grabs (McMichael 2012).

As Borras et al. (2012) point out, however, prevailing approaches to the land grabbing question have tended to highlight certain regions and dimensions to the neglect of others. For instance, studies generally focus on the role of *foreign* companies and *foreign* governments (primarily China, India, South Korea and the Gulf States) in the global land rush. This approach tends to miss or marginalize land grabs carried out by domestic and intra-regional capital, as well as the role of local elites and the state itself (857). Analyses also tend to focus on "mega" deals, measured in terms of *numbers of hectares* grabbed, generally defining a land grab as an acquisition (lease or purchase) greater than 1,000 hectares (850). In a recent presentation, GRAIN (2011b) identifies land grabs as acquisitions of 10,000 hectares or more.

From the point of view of rural people facing eviction and loss of livelihood, it matters little whether the deals in question are for 10,000 hectares or ten. The experience of displacement—whether gradual or sudden, small or large—is one of physical and structural violence, and the end result is community fragmentation and even cultural obliteration. As the agrarian scholar

Aguán peasant stands in front of his destroyed home after an eviction by police, June 2011 (photo by Roger Harris)

Samir Amin (2011) puts it, "we have reached a point at which, in order to open up a new area for capital expansion, it is necessary to destroy entire societies" (xiii).

Along with an emphasis on foreign-led mega-deals, the prevailing approach to land grabs has been Africa-centric. With cases like Ethiopia, where over 1 million hectares of Anuak indigenous lands have been leased to foreign investors (primarily Indian and Saudi), this regional focus clearly is not unwarranted (GRAIN 2010; 2012). But in looking at Latin America, where a different set of dynamics appears to be at work, there is evidence that land grabbing is occurring "to an extent wider than previously assumed" (Borras et al. 2012, 846). The case of the Aguán Valley in northern Honduras, for instance, has been identified in a number of media articles and reports (Oxfam 2011; DanChurchAid 2011) as an emblematic case of land grabbing. And yet, it fits poorly within the model of land grabs outlined above for a number of reasons.

First, the main instance of land grabbing in the Aguán occurred nearly two decades ago, between 1990 and 1994, before the recent food, fuel and financial crises that is widely viewed as triggering the new rush on land. Neoliberal land legislation in 1992 facilitated the process, reversing earlier agrarian reforms and unleashing new investment dynamics that were highly unfavorable to peasant farmers. In a short period, a few wealthy investors seized more than 21,000 hectares (over 70 percent) of peasant lands in the Lower Aguán Valley.

Second, while this would seem to meet the condition of a large-scale land grab, it was not a single transaction, but rather hundreds of small deals, in some cases for less than three hectares. Cumulatively, this flurry of land deals generated widespread peasant dispossession, and concentrated some of the country's best farmland and water resources into a few hands.

Third, the primary actors in the case of the Aguán were not foreign investment firms or transnational agribusiness, but Honduran elites. The biggest investor was Honduran businessman Miguel Facussé Barjum—known as the "richest man in Honduras"—who now controls most of the valley for corporate palm oil production. As part of the "ten families" (as they are commonly known) who now control the country's wealth, Facussé amassed his fortunes with the help of economic policies that liberalized trade and investments—first in manufacturing, and then in agriculture. These policies led to the consolidation of a globally oriented agro-industrial bourgeoisie (see below).

This re-configuration of class power set the stage for a new, intensified phase of agro-industrial expansion beginning in 2009. This phase began with the most all-encompassing and arguably the crudest "grab" of all: the grabbing of state power. The coup that overthrew president Manual Zelaya on June 28, 2009 can be read as the expression of a class process set into motion by neoliberal restructuring. The "new" land grabs in Honduras then, look more like a deepening and intensification of a process already well underway. Put another way, the grabbing of state power is, at least in part, the *political consequence* of an earlier wave of land grabs.[2] Thus, following the work of economic geographer David Harvey (2005), this book argues that neoliberal policies in Honduras should be viewed as a "political project to re-establish the conditions for capital accumulation and to restore the power of economic elites" (19).

Seen in this light, the Honduran case might help us to understand the potential future ramifications of current land grabbing elsewhere.

Neoliberalism and Class Power

Throughout the 20th century, Honduras was known as the quintessential "banana republic" dominated by US agribusiness (e.g. United Fruit) and US military and geopolitical objectives. As historian Walter LaFeber (1984) puts it:

> North American power had become so encompassing that US military forces and United Fruit could struggle against each other to see who was to control the Honduran government, then have the argument settled by the US Department of State. (62)

US capital thus dominated Honduran politics, as well as the most fertile soils and the most lucrative export markets. Comparatively, the Honduran landed elite—which derived its power primarily from enormous ranches and cotton plantations in the South and West—had much less influence. They were, in fact, "the economically poorest and politically weakest rural oligarchy in Central America" (Ruhl 1984, 37).[3]

As Honduran historian Darío Euraque (1996) points out, however, the dominance of US capital in the North did not mean the complete absence of Honduran elites. After World War II, an incipient homegrown bourgeoisie, composed largely of Arab Palestinian immigrants, developed around the northern city of San Pedro Sula, in the heart of the banana-growing Sula Valley. The ethnic composition of this elite class—with Arab surnames like Kattán, Canahuati, Facussé, Násser, Kafati and Larach—was the result of government policies in the early 20th century that promoted foreign immigration as a means to social, cultural and economic progress (González 1992; Foroohar 2011). With the Ottoman Empire in decline, many Palestinian Arabs immigrated to Central America, concentrating in Honduras. While the government hoped these newcomers would develop agriculture, first generation Palestinian immigrants (who intended eventually to return home) rejected the government's land grants and instead gravitated towards commerce, quickly establishing themselves as a powerful merchant class and eventually investing in industry. By the late 1950s, wealthy Palestinian families—often referred to as "Turks" (*los turcos*)—already controlled 75 percent of investments in the import-export sector and about 50 percent of investments in manufacturing (Foroohar 2011).

This "emerging new class of wealth," however, tended to be excluded from political activity partly by their own choice and partly as a result of the unwelcoming attitudes of native Hondurans (Euraque 1996, 35). Structural adjustment policies of the 1990s, however, sparked a massive transfer of state resources to the Honduran private sector, granting north coast-based elites unprecedented access to global markets, investment capital and political power. They expanded their power primarily through two boom sectors of the neoliberal period: manufacturing (*maquilas*) located in over a dozen Export Processing Zones (EPZs) and palm oil based in the Lower Aguán River Valley. A third elite-controlled sector, coastal tourism, flourished in the late 1990s as part of the effort to restructure northern Honduras along investment-friendly lines.

In addition, US-backed militarization in Central America, increasing sharply during the counter-insurgency wars of the 1980s, promoted elite interests by repressing labor unions and peasants associated with the "communist threat." Honduran business and military interests became increasingly intertwined—with one another and with the US—in the 1980s. The anti-communist Association for the Progress of Honduras (APROH) was founded in 1983, with membership comprising all of the country's major businessmen, to promote deregulation, trade liberalization and a military approach to suppressing popular resistance movements

(Envío 1984).[4] Notably, APROH's president was General Gustavo Álvarez Martínez—commander of the armed forces, linked to widespread political assassinations and torture—and its vice-president was businessman Miguel Facussé.

Since the 2009 coup, Honduras has become increasingly militarized. The human rights organization Committee for Relatives of the Detained and Disappeared in Honduras (COFADEH) identifies the current trend as a powerful resurgence of APROH-style authoritarianism: a blend of right-wing extremism, neoliberalism and militarism (Rodríguez 2010). US military aid, ramped up in the name of the War on Drugs, has added fuel to the fire. Efforts have targeted the northern coast and the northeast Moskitia region, areas identified as a "strategic drug trafficking corridor." But the north is also a major area of agribusiness, manufacturing and commercial tourism expansion. US-assisted militarization—combined with the private security forces of large landowners—has been tantamount to an all-out war on peasants, facilitating the expansion of these elite-controlled sectors.

The agro-industrial oligarchy is heavily oriented towards the United States—for trade, investment and cultural cues for looking and acting like a global business elite[5]—and supportive of the US political and economic agenda in Central America. Correspondingly, the US has been instrumental in the *making* of these elites through bilateral and multilateral aid (USAID, IDB) and the policy prescriptions of Washington-based financial institutions (World Bank, IMF). A key moment for the consolidation of the neoliberal model promoted by these institutions was also Hurricane Mitch in 1998. Post-Mitch crisis conditions provided cover for fast-tracking the neoliberal development agenda—focused on the maquila, agroindustry and tourism sectors—newly branded as a plan for "reconstruction" (Boyer and Pell 1999; Jeffrey 1999; Klein 2005; Stonich 2008).

Global market mechanisms, such as those generated by the new "green capitalism," also play a part. Markets for "green" commodities such as crop-based fuel (agrofuels) and carbon credits not only encourage "new" land grabbing, but also add value to *previously* grabbed lands and a sheen of environmental legitimacy. The carbon credits allotted to Miguel Facussé for the greening of palm oil processing, for example, reinforce his ownership claim on highly contested lands in the Aguán.[6] Thus, to say that the 2009 coup and expansion of agro-industrial capital is the result of a "class process" is by no means to dismiss the role of US/Northern imperialism or global capital. Indeed, these forces tend to transform or reinforce local class dynamics in important and historically specific ways.

Grabbing Power (Back)

The land grabs of the 1990s generated a powerful countermovement for the recovery of peasant lands in the Aguán Valley. Dozens of peasant organizations emerged, such as the Peasant Movement of Aguán (MCA) formed in 1999, followed by the Unified Movement of Aguán Peasants (MUCA) in 2001. In most cases, the movements began by pursuing legal strategies— filing requests for the nullification of purchase agreements and demanding investigations of fraudulent deals. When politically influential landowners repeatedly obstructed these approaches, the movements began occupying the oil palm plantations claimed by Facussé and other large landowners. What emerged over a decade of organizing in the Aguán is a mass "grab land back" movement.[7]

This movement made headway under the Zelaya administration (2006-2009), which found itself in an increasingly tense predicament. On one hand was the powerful agro-oligarchy, jealously protecting its newly acquired power and access to foreign investment. On the other hand were 375,000 landless Honduran families, an increasingly militant peasant movement, and steeply rising food prices (Vía Campesina et al. 2011). Faced with these conditions, Zelaya chose to make concessions to social movements, raising the monthly minimum wage and enacting agrarian reform legislation. These policies were met with a growing hostility that foreshadowed the 2009 coup.

Pro-peasant legislation passed by Zelaya was overturned after the coup while the militarization of the countryside further reinforced the power of the agro-oligarchy. US military and development aid quickly resumed, and by November 2010 post-coup president Porfirio "Pepe" Lobo was able to sign agreements with the IMF, IDB and World Bank for $322.5 million to restore the country's economic stability and promote economic growth (Meyer 2010). The Aguán suffered immediate and relentless state-sponsored repression. Between September 2009 and August 2012, there have been 53 recorded cases of peasant murders in the context of the Aguán agrarian conflict—with many more injuries, kidnappings, illegal detentions, forced evictions and cases of torture and sexual assault (FIAN 2012; FIDH 2011; IACHR 2012). Many Aguán peasants and activists now place the death toll at over 60 (Bird 2012).

Paradoxically, the coup inspired a far-reaching political "awakening," as Hondurans often call it. Students, teachers, trade unions, human rights organizations, indigenous peoples, peasants, feminists, LGBT communities, artists, and faith-based groups were galvanized by the coup and the repression that followed, coming

Assembly of the National Front of Popular Resistance (FNRP), February 2011 (photo by Felipe Canova / Creative Commons)

together as the National Front of Resistance Against the Coup (now the National Front of Popular Resistance, or FNRP). In the Aguán Valley, struggles for agrarian reform—a project long tied to the good will of the state—turned into a much more radical struggle to transform state power. The comments of a peasant leader from MUCA in early 2010 are emblematic:

> The people we're fighting against in the Aguán Valley, these are the men who generated poverty for Honduran society and wealth for themselves. And they're the ones who manipulate information, who tell the government what to do and what not to do. They can put a government in power or remove it. So the struggle to liberate the Aguán Valley is a difficult fight, because it's against the entire Honduran oligarchy and also the Honduran government... (Emanuelsson 2010)

Inspired by the struggles of Aguán peasants and the Honduran resistance movement, this book begins from the (perhaps rather obvious) proposition that land grabs are a question of *power*. Thus, in order to understand why they are happening, we must understand 1) how power is historically constituted, and 2) how land grabs further consolidate power in particular ways. Grounded in the historically specific determinants of class, power and land use in northern Honduras, I hope this book contributes to an understanding of the complex forces driving land grabs, particularly in the Americas. Much more ambitiously (and also more urgently) I hope it inspires solidarity and informs strategies to stop them.

This book is the result of over a year and a half of in-depth research—including two fact-finding and solidarity trips to northern Honduras in June 2011 and January 2012—to understand and contextualize the land conflicts in the Aguán. It is based on interviews with peasant and Afro-indigenous community leaders, resistance activists and NGO allies. Because of the lack of available empirical and official data, and the unreliability of prominent media outlets, I relied heavily on first-hand accounts and reports from people on the ground, including interviews, social movement blogs, independent media reports and human rights delegation reports. As much as possible, I confirmed the information contained in this book through more than one source.

The challenge of obtaining and confirming information, however, points to the need for further research, especially from activist researchers willing to assist communities in documenting their own struggles; and from committed journalists willing to highlight the voices and realities of affected communities. For Hondurans, this is a dangerous undertaking indeed: since the coup, at least 22 Honduran media workers have been murdered for daring to break the silence of elite-managed censorship (UNESCO 2012). While this violence is chilling, it shows that even an authoritarian state depends on a modicum of legitimacy, which it can only ensure by suppressing the right to free expression. The role of the US government in funding this repression with taxpayer dollars confers upon US citizens a special responsibility and capacity to act. While this book aims to contribute to the body of scholarship on Honduras and agrarian struggles, it is also a call for international solidarity with the Honduran resistance and the peasants of the Aguán.

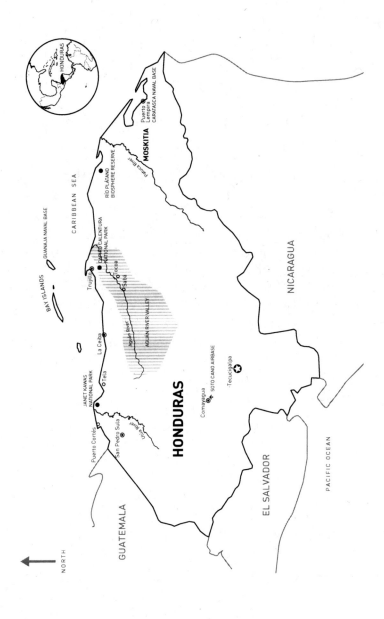

PART 1

FROM BANANAS TO PALM OIL

Known as the quintessential "banana republic", Honduras is no stranger to agribusiness. At the turn of the twentieth century, US companies took over large swaths of fertile land for plantation fruit production. These companies also exerted extraordinary power over domestic politics. The first president to be installed by banana interests in 1912, Manuel Bonilla repealed a two cents per stem tax on banana exports and made large land concessions to the fruit companies. By 1917 a few foreign firms led by United Fruit (now Chiquita Brands) owned almost a million acres of the best Honduran farmland (LaFeber 1984, 178). Most of these lands are on the Atlantic coast, a water-abundant region with 13 river basins, producing 87 percent of the country's surface water (USAID 2011b). United Fruit's far-reaching control over land, resources and political power in Central America earned it the nickname *el pulpo*, "the octopus."

As Alison Acker (1988) points out in her book *The Making of a Banana Republic*, "there was no real land shortage for the Honduran peasant until the twentieth century" (90). In a mountainous country with only one fifth of its land suitable for agriculture (Barry 1991: 308), the expansion of export agriculture and cattle ranching quickly displaced peasant food production, pushing it onto poor soils and steep hillsides, deepening rural poverty. The fast rise of corporate fruit empires sparked militant movements of peasants and plantation workers fighting for the right to land. While these struggles achieved important reforms, they were insufficient to solve the country's deep land inequality and rural poverty. The overthrow of president Manuel Zelaya Rosales on June 28, 2009, supported by the country's landowning and business elite, ushered in yet a new phase of agro-industrial expansion and peasant repression.

In the Aguán region, a fertile alluvial valley just south of the northern coast, large landowners have taken advantage of the current political climate to intensify attacks on peasant movements and expand plantations of African oil palm, a high value export crop with a growing global market for edible oil, processed foods, chemicals and biodiesel. Between September 2009 and August 2012, 53 recorded murders of Aguán peasants are attributed to guards and mercenaries hired by large oil palm growers, often acting in concert with state police and military forces (FIAN 2012; IACHR 2012). In addition, the US military presence and military aid—heightened in recent years in the name of the combatting drug trafficking—have bolstered Honduran security forces' capacity for repression. The revival of 1980s-style counter-insurgency tactics against a non-violent resistance movement has led to mounting human rights atrocities felt most acutely in the countryside. This push also comes up against a movement of increasingly organized peasant communities who, after more than a century of displacement by capitalist agriculture, have nowhere left to go.

Part One traces the history of agro-industry in Honduras, from the "banana republic" to the rise of the new palm oil oligarchy. This history largely unfolds in the valleys and coastal areas of Northern Honduras, a region with the country's most fertile soils, access to Central America's largest deep-water port, and strategic importance in the increasingly militarized War on Drugs. The first chapter begins in the Aguán Valley, a region that once offered the promise of a better life for thousands of peasant families and continues to represent a powerful alternative vision of "land for the people."

1
THE AGUÁN VALLEY:
LAND FOR THE PEOPLE

The development of the Aguán has its roots in state-led agrarian reform policies of the 1960s and 70s that designated these lands for the collective use of the peasantry. The peasants who benefitted from these reforms nonetheless had to fight to improve living conditions and gain greater control over the value of their labor. This history of struggle has created a strong sense of peasant identity and entitlement to land in the Aguán.

In the 1950s, the North American fruit companies' stranglehold on the Honduran economy met with increasingly organized resistance by plantation workers over land, wages, working conditions and collective bargaining rights. In May 1954, a series of strikes broke out along the northern coast against United Fruit that rapidly spread to other industries, reaching nearly 30,000 workers (Merrill 1995). The general strike of 1954 became a watershed moment in Honduran social history. The two largest companies, Standard Fruit and United Fruit, responded by mechanizing production and firing half of their workforce by 1959 (Acker 1988, 67).[8] This only augmented the mass of people clamoring for land, creating a powerful movement of peasants and landless workers that the government was forced to reckon with. The modern peasant movement in Honduras is rooted in these historic labor struggles against US fruit companies in the mid-20th century:

> Enraged at their dismissal and with few economic alternatives available to them, many of the former fruit company employees took over company lands to begin subsistence farming. They were transformed almost immediately from an angry proletarian labor force into an angry landless peasant work force. Growing agitation among former fruit company workers spread to peasant groups across the nation. (Nelson 2003, 7)

In the eyes of the United States, these increasingly unruly peasants made Honduras vulnerable to communism, a grave threat to US corporate interests. In Guatemala, an attempt to solve the land question by redistributing United Fruit lands to the peasantry led to the removal of president Jacobo Arbenz via a CIA-assisted coup in 1954. In Honduras, the US took a different approach. The Kennedy administration launched the short-lived Alliance for Progress Initiative, signed at the Inter-American Congress in Punta del Este, Uruguay in 1961. The Charter called for a reformist approach to quelling social unrest in the US's "backyard" through social programs, development aid and agrarian reform. Similarly, the US Agency for International Development (USAID) and the Peace Corps were also created under Kennedy's watch, to promote US interests abroad through non-military means (albeit side by side with military means).[9]

The success of the 1959 Cuban revolution in challenging US imperialism and redistributing land to the peasantry inspired a dramatic growth in demands for social change throughout Latin America. With the Alliance for Progress, the US hoped reform would stem the tide of revolution by fostering a "development state" to attend to social demands. The reforms supported by the Alliance, however, were far from revolutionary. Predictably, they did not touch the large landholdings of US fruit companies. Rather, the reform law signed in 1961 promoted a "colonization" of the agricultural frontier (rainforest) by peasants and landless workers. As if to reassure US patrons, then-president Villeda Morales declared: "This [reform] is neither communist nor socialist; it is a purely liberal and democratic agrarian reform that will not take away any lands from *latifundistas*" (FOSDEH et al. n.d., 14).

The state-owned lands of the Aguán Valley in the northern department of Colón became one of the reform's main colonization sites, now known as the "reform sector."[10] The colonization of Aguán with poor peasants from around the country was a difficult process with a high abandonment rate. Initial failures required the State to adopt a more integrated development strategy beyond simply doling out parcels of undeveloped rainforest. In 1970, the National Agrarian Institute (INA) began actively promoting the creation of cooperatively run "peasant enterprises" (*empresas campesinas*).[11] Through the cooperative structure, peasant settlers received state support in the form of inputs, credit, price supports and infrastructure to grow bananas, citrus and especially oil palm fruit for sale to the US fruit companies or to new state-owned palm processors.

African oil palm (*Elaeis guineensis*) was introduced to Honduras by United Fruit in the early twentieth century as an experimental crop. At the time, the rapid spread of Fusarium wilt, dubbed "Panama disease", was devastating the company's banana plantations throughout Central American and the Caribbean. The company tried to stay ahead of the fungus by abandoning diseased plantations and taking over new areas, such as the forested lands of the upper Ulúa Valley of Honduras; Tiquisate, Guatemala; and Quepos, Costa Rica (Marquardt 2001). It also tried beating the disease by exerting greater control over nature through industrialization—dredging canals, applying chemicals and researching new crop varieties—drastically transforming both the landscape and the labor processes. By 1948, the company boasted: "Virtually overnight, tens of thousands of machete swingers have become spray men, mechanics, tractor operators and technicians. This is the significant achievement of the last 20 years: control" (quoted in Marquardt 2001).

Despite these triumphal claims, Panama disease continued to spread, forcing United Fruit to experiment with new crops.

The company created the Department of Tropical Research in La Lima, Honduras in 1923 and the Lancetilla Experiment Station near Tela in 1926 to import genetic material and perform trials with oil palm and other tropical substitutes for bananas (Richardson 1995). It was only in the late 1960s, however, that major breakthroughs were made (in pollination, fertilization and oil extraction techniques) allowing for the large-scale commercial planting of oil palm in Latin America (see Part Two).

Since the US fruit companies had not yet gained monopoly control over the incipient palm oil industry, the Honduran government was able to enter the market in 1970, using the product as a development tool for the reform sector. African oil palm thus became the hallmark crop for the development of the Aguán, particularly within the fertile river basin east of Sabá, an area known as "Lower Aguán" (*Bajo Aguán*).

The Inter-American Development Bank (IDB) funded the Aguán project as the basis for industrial development, since oil palm production would generate the need for crushing mills, refineries and final-goods factories (DeFontenay 1999). Through a combination of IDB loans and bilateral aid (primarily from

Harvested palm fruit on an Aguán plantation (photo by Jesse Freeston)

the UK and the Netherlands), the state constructed a 500-kilometer road network in the Aguán, three palm processing plants and a modern port (ibid.). Hoping to pay down its large debts, primarily to the IDB, the state-controlled processing plants bought palm fruit at measly prices. According to DeFontenay (1999), "Regardless of how much palm they delivered, cooperatives were paid 3 lempiras [approximately US$1.50] per day per member, which was near or below the going wage for agricultural day-laborers."

In return for accepting such low earnings, peasant cooperatives were promised eventual control over the state-owned processing board, Coapalma. This promise was only fulfilled after a 17-day peasant strike in 1981 that brought production to a grinding halt, finally winning peasants control over the processing and marketing of their product (Macías 2001, 83).

Even though it occurred on the back of state-led agrarian reform, the development of the Aguán was clearly not intended to support peasant autonomy or local food production. Rather, it aimed to "modernize" smallholders by incorporating them into agro-export production. Locked into production contracts with Coapalma, Standard Fruit and other firms, they had limited sovereignty over their land use decisions.

Aguán settlers did in fact cultivate food. Gould (1986) describes how the Aguán co-ops assigned individual plots to each family for the production of corn and beans for consumption, which were grown without pesticides or fertilizers (compared to input-intensive oil palm) (ibid.). But policy makers saw peasant subsistence as an obstacle to development instead of a desirable outcome—a view strongly reinforced by international aid agencies then and now. This helps to explain why by the 1990s, the co-ops were widely seen as a failure: Aguán peasants were still producing far too much food and not enough oil palm to keep the processing plants competitive. By 1993, only 30 percent of the Aguán Valley's land area was planted to project-promoted cash crops (half of which consisted of oil palm) compared to 50 percent in neighboring Sula Valley (DeFontenay 1999).

Still, the development state of the 1970s took precautions to ensure reformed lands would benefit the poor and not the rich. A 1974 law (Decree Law 170) placed limits on the size of large properties and prohibited their sale, requiring that they be reverted to the state for re-distribution to landless peasants. In conjunction with the original 1961 agrarian reform law, this new legislation was critical to protecting Aguán lands for the benefit of rural families.

Over three decades of agrarian reform, 409,000 hectares were awarded to 60,000 families, covering 12.3 percent of the country's total agricultural land (FIAN 2000). Waves of poor migrants drawn to the Aguán in the 1970s, primarily from the south of the country, worked tirelessly in harsh tropical conditions in the hopes of a better life—building infrastructure, clearing the forest and preparing the land. Consequently, Aguán peasants have a strong feeling of collective pride over the region's development, which they see as the result of 1) their historic struggle for agrarian reform and 2) the blood, sweat and tears they have poured into these lands for multiple generations.

2
THE DECLINE OF AGRICULTURE
AND THE RISE OF THE MAQUILA

The 1980s saw the end of state-led development and the beginning of an era of free market economics and neoliberal ideology. These policies removed state supports for agriculture, unleashing new trade and investment dynamics that left smallholders extremely vulnerable to dispossession. This parallels the rapid rise of the manufacturing sector, which could absorb the desperate flow of people from the countryside—especially women—into its workforce.

Like many countries of the Global South, the legacy of foreign debt has crippled Honduran democracy, orienting macroeconomic policies towards debt repayment instead of local development. By the end of the 1980s, Honduras was in the full throes of the Latin American debt crisis, with an external debt totaling $3 billion in 1989—nearly 70 percent of the country's GDP (World Bank 1995). The World Bank and International Monetary Fund (IMF) stepped in to provide debt restructuring conditioned upon the implementation of far-reaching austerity measures to cut public spending and increase foreign exchange revenues (ibid.). The Honduran Structural Adjustment Program (SAP) included the typical combination of privatization, liberalization and deflationary monetary policy.

One of the first adjustment policies enacted by president Rafael Leonardo Callejas (1990-1994) was the devaluation of the national currency (lempira) in order to stimulate exports and improve the country's balance of payments.[12] Export-promotion favored large producers, such as the transnational fruit companies, selling to the external market. On top of this, the "Law of Incentives for Banana Production" passed in May 1991 offered three-year tax exemptions for all new banana cultivation and reduced taxes on banana exports (Thorpe 2002, 79).

The impact of structural adjustment on smallholders, however, was brutal. Small and medium producers buying inputs with a weakened lempira found their production costs rising and their profits plummeting. The privatization of the National Agricultural Marketing Board (IHMA) in February 1991 slashed regulations on grain imports and exports. It also eliminated price guarantees for staples like corn, beans, rice, chicken and milk, leaving both farmers and consumers at the mercy of the global market. These policies coincided with the liberalization of agricultural trade at the regional level with the approval of the Action Plan for Central American Agriculture (PAC) in July 1991, leading to the elimination of trade barriers on 12 basic agricultural products (Thorpe 2002).[13]

As a result, total agricultural imports grew by over 16 percent per year between 1990 and 2000, devastating the basic grains sector and transforming consumption patterns (FAO 2003). During this period, Hondurans "moved from making their own flour and tortillas using their domestic production of white maize, to importing a substantial amount of breakfast cereals and processed cereals" (ibid.).

The collapse of smallholder agriculture led to a flood of out-migration, disrupting family structures and community life in the countryside. Remittances from migrant workers abroad—87 percent of who live in the United States—have become the largest single source of foreign exchange for Honduras, amounting to 20 percent of GDP in 2008 (Meyer 2011, 21). As droves of (primarily) young men from the countryside headed for the US in search of work, those who stayed behind (especially women) sought employment in the booming manufacturing (*maquila*) sector.

Aided by trade liberalization and the creation of more than twenty Export Processing Zones, or EPZs,—areas where manufacturing firms operate tax-free—the Honduran maquila boom is dominated by investments from the United States. In 2003, only 17 percent of garment workers were employed by Honduran firms; the largest employers were US companies (53 percent) followed by South Korean companies (15 percent) (Marcouiller and Robertson 2009). High levels of foreign ownership, however, did not prevent an incipient class of Honduran industrialists (tied to transnational capital) from also making windfall profits.

Mario Canahuati—former ambassador to the US (2002-2005) and now foreign minister under the Lobo government—made his fortunes in the maquila sector. Even in his current government position, Canahuati remains as director of the Lovable Group, one of the largest industrial groups in Central America. Today, Lovable owns four EPZs that manufacture products for Costco, Hanes, Russell Athletic, Footlocker, JC Penny and Sara Lee (Paley 2010). Canahuati is also a prominent member (and former president) of the Honduran Council of Private Enterprises (COHEP), a group that strongly condemned Zelaya's minimum wage increase,[14] and publicly applauded the June 2009 coup (La Tribuna 2008; COHEP 2009; El Heraldo 2009a).

Now the fifth largest supplier of clothing products in the world, the Honduran textile industry is touted as a neoliberal success story. But Honduran competitiveness and high profits mask atrocious labor conditions, poverty-level wages and an extremely vulnerable workforce composed primarily of rural women and girls, 70 percent of whom are between the ages of 18 and 25 (Oxfam 2008). Maquila workers are generally prohibited from forming unions and subjected to pervasive gender discrimination, sexual violence, forced sterilization, and gender-based killings or "femicide"—a phenomenon widely linked to the emergence of manufacturing zones in Central America and on the northern Mexico border (Prieto-Carrón et al. 2007). Women maquila workers, many of whom are single mothers and their family's sole breadwinner, are often fired by the age

BOX 1. WOMEN MAQUILA WORKERS RESIST

In the face of entrenched patriarchy—in the home, workplace and traditional labor unions—women maquila workers have organized powerful organizations, such as the Honduran Women's Collective (CODEMUH), to fight for better living and working conditions. CODEMUH has not only achieved important victories in the factories—such as workers' compensation for occupational injuries and diseases—it has also increased women's participation in political advocacy. In March 2008, CODEMUH presented a proposal to the Zelaya government to reform the country's outdated labor code. According to María Luisa Regalado (2011), General Coordinator of CODEMUH, "it was the first time that a grassroots feminist organization in Honduras [had] written and presented a workers' rights proposal for legislative reform." The proposed law was passed by the national congress, but any further progress was stalled by the coup. Despite the setback, and the post-coup climate of repression, CODEMUH's work continues. Regalado continues:

> The National Front [of Popular Resistance] has incorporated our legislative occupational health and safety reform in its agenda, ensuring the support of several trade unions and grassroots organizations in the struggle to improve health and safety legislation... We know that there is still much to do. Governments like the one in Honduras continue to allow multinational corporations to exploit the health of the working population with impunity. But we will continue to demand justice and organize workers to call for the respect of human, labor and gender rights.

of 35, becoming "surplus populations" searching for informal work and living in extreme poverty on the outskirts of industrial towns (Oxfam 2008).[15]

Nonetheless, the feminization of industrial labor also led to the emergence of strong organizations working to build class and feminist consciousness among Honduran maquila workers (See Box 1).

As the manufacturing sector and remittance economy increased dramatically during the "adjustment decade," agriculture took a nosedive. Whereas food imports accounted for 10-12 percent of foreign exchange earnings in the mid-1980s, that number more than tripled by the year 2000, reaching 36 percent (FAO 2003). This reliance on foreign markets is especially skewed towards the United States, the country's largest supplier of both food imports and industrial inputs for manufacturing, creating a relationship of dependence further deepened by the Central American-Dominican Republic Free Trade Agreement (CAFTA-DR) passed by Honduras in 2006 (see Part Two). To meet its rising food imports bill, the country is now highly dependent on foreign exchange from the manufacturing sector and remittances, a condition of structural dependence difficult to overcome.

There are clear correlations between the decline of peasant agriculture and the rise of the maquila sector and out-migration. Between 1990 and 2006, the proportion of the population living in rural areas fell from 60 percent to 54 percent, and the number of landless families more than doubled—from approximately 126,000 to 300,000 (Nelson 2003; USAID 2011). During the same period, employment in Honduran maquilas increased from approximately 19,400 to 106,500 workers—from 1.3 percent to 4.4 percent of the working population (De Hoyos et al. 2008). The number of Hondurans living in the United States during this period also increased. There are now approximately 428,000 Honduran-born migrants in the US, 79 percent of whom arrived after 1990 (Meyer 2012).

In sum, neoliberal policies shifted the Honduran economy

away from agriculture, especially the production of basic food-
stuffs, to a new emphasis on manufacturing and export-led
growth. The displacement of peasants from agriculture generated
a pool of exploitable surplus labor for the burgeoning maquila
sector. The articulation of these two sectors—agricultural and
industrial—is key to understanding the forces behind agrarian
change in Honduras (and elsewhere). It also points to the kinds
of political alliances (rural-urban, peasant-worker, local-global)
likely needed to effect meaningful structural change.

3
GRABBING LAND AND POWER: THE NEW AGRO-OLIGARCHS

Neoliberalism set the stage for a massive re-concentration of land in the Aguán into the hands of a few influential elites. Like the industrialists of the maquila sector, these individuals were well positioned to benefit from newly liberalized markets in land, trade and investment. The primary mechanism through which this land grab took place was the Agricultural Modernization Law (AML),[16] conceived by the international financial institutions and enacted in 1992, privatizing collective landholdings. The peasant cooperatives of the Aguán—located on some of the country's richest land—were all but annihilated in a short period. The result has been the consolidation of a small class of agro-industrial elite with control over most of the valley and strong ties to transnational capital.

SAP-mandated privatization policies generated a tremendous transfer of resources from the public to the private sector. Businessman Miguel Facussé Barjum, now the richest man in Honduras, amassed part of his fortune through the dissolution of the Honduran National Investment Bank (CONADI) in 1990, which had loaned millions to his manufactured goods companies (Galaxia and Químicas Dinant). With the help of this infusion of capital, Facussé quickly began buying up the Aguán Valley and northern coast, from Tela in the West to Río Plátano in the East. Struggling under the weight of debt, low returns and rising input costs, highly vulnerable Aguán peasants were susceptible to these buyouts.

The hardest blow came with the implementation of land tenure "modernization," shorthand for privatizing and individualizing land titles so that they could be bought and sold on the free market. As part of the broader program of neoliberal reforms, the 1992 AML—also known as the "Norton Law" for its author, USAID economist Roger Norton—was the death knell of agrarian reform. It represented a shift from a national "land to the tiller" paradigm to a so-called "willing buyer–willing seller" paradigm promoted by the World Bank.[17]

In fact, the privatization of land began well before the AML through a USAID-funded land-titling program initiated in 1982. Between 1982 and 1991, the program granted 37,174 individual titles, primarily to smallholders, covering 319,311 hectares of land (Nelson 2003). The program received high praises from large landowners and from then-US Ambassador John Negroponte, who praised the program for making "owners of hundreds of peasant families, persons who can now look for resources to obtain credit and technical support, very important aspects for the advancement of the agricultural sector in Honduras" (Jansen and Roquas 1998, 86). Jansen and Roquas' (1998) study, however, shows that land titling heightened local land conflicts and did little to improve access to credit or tenure security for the poor.

Up until 1992, the Aguán Valley was excluded from land titling programs since the government prohibited the sale or lease of lands acquired through agrarian reform. The AML, however, reversed these prohibitions, legalizing the private transfer of Aguán lands and permitting the piecemeal sale of cooperatives. With the cooperatives already hurting, this abrupt liberalization of the land market led to a dramatic sell-off of peasant land in the Aguán. These "voluntary" sales were helped along through varying degrees of intimidation and manipulation: from bribes to peasant leaders, to menacing letters from INA, to violent threats from large landowners (MUCA 2010a).

As Thorpe (2002) points out, it is difficult to distinguish between a "forced" and a "voluntary" land sale in this context.

Many cooperatives sold their land out of extreme distress: "The Uchapita cooperative in Aguán, for instance, sold all its 77 hectares for a reported price of 134,750 lempiras [approximately US$24,900], yet its outstanding debts were estimated to be in the order of 300,000 lempiras [approximately US$55,500]" (337).

Facussé and other investors—members of the privileged political class that had promoted SAPs—began chipping away at cooperative lands, buying up properties at fire-sale prices. Peasants who sold lands before deflation went into effect quickly saw their newfound cash devalued by more than half (Bolpress 2011). By 1994, approximately 30,500 hectares (over 75,000 acres) of "reform sector" lands—state-owned lands reserved for the collective use of the peasantry—were bought by private investors (FOSDEH et al. n.d., 30). The land transfers occurred in resource-rich parts of the country: areas with fertile soils; water resources; and access to communication, energy and transport infrastructure (i.e. infrastructure financed by external debt and built up during the development decades). Thus, the fertile Aguán region suffered the highest levels of land re-concentration in the country.

Aguán peasant workers load palm fruit onto a tractor-trailer (photo by Jesse Freeston)

While the national average for land re-concentration between 1990 and 1994 was less than 10 percent, in the Aguán Valley and Atlantic coast regions—areas suitable for high-value crops like bananas, sugarcane and oil palm—more than 70 percent was re-concentrated (COCOCH n.d., 149). Of the 28,365 hectares (approximately 70,000 acres) awarded to peasant cooperatives by the agrarian reform in Aguán, 20,930 (nearly three quarters) were grabbed in a short period (ibid.). With a few exceptions (see the case of Salamá in Part Three), the Aguán cooperative sector was decimated. A total of 40 peasant-owned oil palm cooperatives lost their lands (MUCA 2010b). Three Honduran oil palm investors were the primary beneficiaries: Miguel Facussé, René Morales Carazo and Reinaldo Canales.

The transnational fruit companies also expanded their production area during this period. In 1990, for example, Standard Fruit acquired the lands of Isletas, a banana-producing peasant cooperative in Olanchito seen as one of the beacons of agrarian reform in the Aguán region. Thorpe (2002) argues that this expansion was made possible by a combination of the AML and policies favoring agro-export promotion (see chapter 2).

Miguel Facussé, however, is the central figure in land struggles in the Aguán and throughout the country (Mejía 2011). Propelled by structural adjustment and foreign investments, Facussé has become one of a handful of recognizable surnames in Honduras—the "ten families" as they are popularly known—with control over the country's wealth and political system (Vos el Soberano 2009). His companies in diverse sectors—from food to energy to tourism—have become a veritable "octopus" rivaling the historic power of United Fruit. His private security guards have been linked to dozens of peasant murders, crimes that go unpunished because of his close ties to the political establishment and business community.[18]

This emergence of a powerful agro-oligarchy in Northern Honduras is novel. Unlike neighboring El Salvador, where a few wealthy families "made fortunes in coffee during the nineteenth century then moved to take control of trade and banking, the

Hondurans never took that first step of gaining some control over their nation's key product [bananas]" (LaFeber 1984, 43). The US corporate monopoly over bananas (and the best lands) in the north blocked Honduran capital from entering the lucrative export enclave. The country's landed elite was located primarily in the south, on large cattle ranches, but had long been dwarfed by the political power of US capital. Honduran governments, notes Ruhl (1984) "basically represented the interests of the North American banana companies and of whichever political faction was dominant at the moment rather than the interests of the cattlemen." Structural adjustment, however, allowed Honduran investors to appropriate the state-created palm oil sector, building up the presence of domestic capital in northern agribusiness. Additionally, the Honduran oligarchy used the crisis created by Hurricane Mitch in 1998 to further tighten its hold on power (See Box 2).

In addition to privatization, the liberalization of trade and investments facilitated a slew of mergers, acquisitions and co-investments that incorporated national companies like Facussé's into the supply chains of powerful transnational firms. Both Unilever and Proctor & Gamble, for instance, gained important footholds in Central America by acquiring distribution networks and brands owned by Facussé. By buying his Cressida Corporation (including patents on soaps, beverages and processed foods) for $314 million in 2000, Unilever doubled its presence in Central America (Unilever 2000). Facussé retained control of Cressida's Aguán palm plantations and a number of snack food brands, now under the name Dinant. One of the biggest players in the palm oil trade, Unilever uses around 1.2 million tons of palm oil every year (Greenpeace 2007).

The rise of Facussé mirrors the consolidation of class power in many countries during the neoliberal period. As Harvey (2005) notes, between 1994 and 1998, "the world's 200 richest people more than doubled their net worth to more than $1 trillion. The assets of the top three billionaires were by then more than the combined GNP of all least developed countries and their

600 million people" (35). Indonesia—incidentally the world's leading oil palm producer—offers a striking parallel. With a net worth of $3.6 billion, Anthony Salim controls the Salim Group, Indonesia's largest conglomerate with stakes in the food and beverage industry, food processing, oil palm plantations, shopping centers, real estate and resort-style tourism (Jakarta Post 2012). Like Facussé, Salim (with close ties to dictator Suharto) amassed tremendous wealth under a neoliberal regime backed by a strong military.

To summarize, neoliberal policies not only reversed the state-led development paradigm of the 1960s and 70s, replacing it with a free-market model. They also *transferred* the tremendous physical capital built up during the development decades in the Aguán—roads, ports, processing plants and oil palm plantations—into the hands of a few wealthy families.[19] In so doing, the many fruits of debt-financed "development" ostensibly meant for the public good were appropriated for private profit (i.e. privatized). This facilitated the rise of a new agro-oligarchy in northern Honduras linked like never before, thanks to liberalization and to transnational capital and finance.

The new, globally integrated Honduran oligarchy—based largely in the maquila and palm oil sectors—gained unprecedented power (and motive) to further restructure domestic politics in favor of capitalist expansion. The 2009 coup can be read, in part, as the logical outcome of this new configuration of class power.

BOX 2. HURRICANE MITCH: DISASTER CAPITALISM AND GRASSROOTS ALTERNATIVES

When Hurricane Mitch hit Central America in October 1998, Honduras was already highly vulnerable—socially and ecologically. Many point out that Mitch was far from a mere "natural" disaster. Decades of US-backed agro-export development had monopolized the country's best farmland, forcing droves of rural poor into environmentally at-risk areas: fragile soils, steep hillsides and urban slums. Perched on Tegucigalpa's outskirts or along Choluteca's deforested riverbanks, whole neighborhoods were washed away by the storm. In the northern floodplains, dominated by banana and oil palm plantations, "massive flooding drowned countless people and stranded thousands of workers on the tin roofs of their banana camps for days without food or drinking water" (Boyer and Pell 1999, 39). Mitch killed an estimated 6,500 people and left 1.5 million people displaced or homeless, in a country of 6 million (NCDC 2009).

Immediately after the storm, the government of Carlos Flores Facussé (1998-2002) declared martial law, dissolved civil liberties and created a special commission to carry out a top-down emergency response plan (Stonich 2008, 55). The authoritarian response, notes Jeffrey (1998), emerged from a fear that the poor would become so desperate as to revolt against the country's extreme class divisions. It also helped to consolidate the neoliberal model and deepen elite power. In the throes of crisis, the Honduran congress fast-tracked its privatization agenda, rapidly selling off airports, seaports and highways and introducing laws to privatize public utilities such as the state-owned telephone and electric companies (Klein 2005). Companies like Chiquita used production losses as an excuse to lay off thousands of unionized workers, later replacing them with non-union workers (Boyer and Pell 1999, 40).

While magnifying inequality, these policies helped demonstrate fiscal discipline and attract international aid. At the International Summit for Central American Reconstruction in Stockholm, donors committed $2.7 billion in loans and grants for Honduran reconstruction (ibid.). But "reconstruction" reflected the neoliberal government's pre-Mitch priorities: expanding maquilas, strengthening agro-industry and opening up coastal areas for tourism (Jeffrey 1999; Stonich 2008). In a textbook example of what Naomi Klein (2005; 2007) calls "disaster capitalism" the government and financial institutions used the hurricane to aggressively push this agenda through.

For civil society, however, the hurricane exposed an intense vulnerability rooted in inequality, and in some cases gave rise to new forms of grassroots organizing. In Aguán, neoliberal policies had destroyed the peasant cooperative sector, but a strong ethic of collective organization remained. Faced with the need to care for survivors and rebuild after the storm, Aguán peasants and coastal Afro-indigenous peoples formed Local Emergency Committees (CODELs) with support from the Catholic Church (Envío 2000; Jeffrey 2002). The CODELs organized relief efforts and demanded participation in the government's allocation of emergency funds. By mobilizing local labor, the CODELs restored over 6,400 homes, 186 kilometers of drainage ditches; 37 small bridges; 530 hygienic garbage dumps; 47 community water systems; 4,500 acres of corn and bean fields; and planted 30,000 saplings in buffer zones to protect watersheds (Envío 2000). In contrast to the male-dominated cooperatives and patronatos (local governing councils), women had a strong role as organizers and leaders in the CODELs.

In April 1999, 700 landless peasants, many of whom had been active in CODELs, formed the Peasant Movement of Aguán (MCA) (see Part Three). The following month, MCA launched the large-scale occupation of a former military training site, organizing teams to supervise health, food production, security and education. Unlike earlier peasant organizations, women shared equally in the movement's leadership (Jeffrey 2002, 48). In February 2000, 84 CODELs gathered in a massive town hall forum in the town of Tocoa—a grassroots alternative to the Stockholm Summit—to discuss "the kind of values that should underpin the new Honduran society" (Envío 2000). Thus, while the rich used the hurricane as an opportunity for "disaster capitalism," Mitch also sparked a broader awareness of ecological vulnerability and structural inequality. It may have even sparked the beginnings of the current resistance movement. Aguán community leader Lorenzo Cruz commented, "The Lower Aguán Valley can be a sign of hope for Honduras; it's a sign of what's possible with real democracy" (Jeffrey 2002, 50).

4
MILITARIZATION AND THE WAR ON DRUGS: SECURITY FOR WHOM?

Throughout the twentieth century, the United States protected its national and corporate interests in Central America through repeated military interventions. With Roosevelt's 1904 corollary to the Monroe Doctrine, the US came to see itself as the "policeman" of the western hemisphere, with the special responsibility of protecting the small isthmian nations of Central America from would-be aggressors (identified at different times as Spain, Britain, the Soviet Union, Cuba and now Venezuela) (LaFeber 1984). In the present-day context of the War on Drugs—and with far fewer US allies in Latin America—Honduras remains strategically important to US geopolitical interests in the region.

Honduras solidified its role as the strategic outpost of the United States in the 1980s, when it became the base for military and intelligence operations against the leftist Sandinista government of Nicaragua. The US provided roughly $1.6 billion in economic and military aid to Honduras during that decade as part of its counter-insurgency effort in Central America, establishing 1,200 troops at Soto Cano (formerly Palmerola) Airbase near the capital Tegucigalpa through Joint Task Force (JTF) Bravo (Meyer 2011). Over this period, around 9,500 Honduran military officials were trained at the US Army School of the Americas (moved from Panama to Fort Benning, Georgia in 1985) (Barry and Norsworthy 1991, 334). Additionally, "Mobile Training

Teams" of US Special Forces (Green Berets) in Honduras trained entire units in counterinsurgency tactics (ibid.).

While enlisted by the US to carry out operations against its neighbors, Honduras in the 1980s was guided by the principles of the US national security doctrine (NSD). Associated with "dirty wars" throughout the hemisphere, NSD entailed a reorientation of the military project *inward*, targeting anyone in the country thought to be "subversive" in order to counter soviet influence—whether real or perceived. In practice this often meant attacking labor unions, peasant associations, student groups and other popular organizations (Barry and Norsworthy 1991). Between 1982 and 1984, in the initial wave of systematic repression, the Honduran military carried out 214 political assassinations, 110 forced disappearances and 1,947 illegal detentions (297).

The Honduran military remains a powerful institution, strongly allied to US interests. JTF Bravo maintains a presence of approximately 600 troops at Soto Cano, which serves as

President Barack Obama (right) meets with Honduran president Porfirio "Pepe" Lobo in the Oval Office of the White House, October 2011 (photo by Charles Dharapak / AP)

the central coordinating authority for US military activities in Central America and beyond. The military overthrow of president Manuel Zelaya on June 28, 2009—and the all-too-familiar repression of civil society that followed—raised serious questions about ongoing US militarization, security aid, tactical support and training for the Honduran military.

While the US suspended most joint military activities and aid after the coup,[20] military cooperation fully resumed after the election of coup supporter Porfirio Lobo, who has taken aggressive measures to court US investors with new business-friendly policies. Through the National Investment Promotion Plan (2010-2014) and related legislation, Lobo seeks to position Honduras as "the most attractive investment destination in Latin America."[21] This includes providing tax breaks and other incentives for agribusiness, extractive industries (mining and forestry), tourism, renewable energy (agrofuels and mega-dams) and manufacturing zones.[22]

Oddly, neither Zelaya nor his Liberal Party had been particularly hostile to foreign investment.[23] It was under Zelaya's watch in 2006 that Honduras joined CAFTA-DR, which eliminated most remaining barriers to US investments and imports. Zelaya also passed biofuels legislation in November 2007, the first of its kind in Central America, supporting increased foreign investments in agricultural biofuels (Trucchi 2008). Despite a great deal of fear mongering from the business elite—associating Zelaya with the Venezuelan "red threat"—the 2009 coup actually replaced a *reformist,* pro-investment administration with an *extremist* one.

Reforms under Zelaya included raising the minimum wage; engaging in negotiations with peasant movements; legalizing emergency contraception for women; and joining the Venezuela-led oil cartel Petrocaribe to relieve fuel prices (a move now supported by the Lobo government) (Prensa Latina 2011). More than these policies, however, popular demands for a new constituent assembly—to redraft the 1982 constitution passed under highly militarized conditions—were among the biggest threats to elite power. In response to broad-based organizing by social movements, Zelaya had agreed to hold a national referendum, scheduled for June 28, 2009, asking citizens to vote on convening a constituent assembly.[24] The coup occurred on the morning of the referendum, sending a clear message about the oligarchy's disdain for popular consultation. Since then, the redrafting of the constitution to "re-found" Honduras along more democratic and participatory lines remains the central unifying issue for the diverse coalition of groups opposing the coup.

Without dismissing US involvement, the 2009 coup appears to have been orchestrated primarily by the Honduran bourgeoisie, fearful of an erosion of its class position. Of course, for the US, support for the new business-friendly regime did not stray far from past policies in Central America. Along with security aid, US development aid resumed in early 2010, including new "food security" funds meant to both stabilize the post-coup government and open the door to US companies like Wal-Mart (See Box 4).

The US War on Drugs also escalated after the coup, following the Mexican and Colombian models of militarization. The Central American Security Initiative (CARSI, formerly Plan Mérida) received $260 million in congressional appropriations between 2008 and 2010, and another $100 million requested for 2012 (Meyer 2011). This was part of a larger military expansion plan including $25 million to upgrade Soto Cano Airbase with new permanent barracks, and two newly expanded Atlantic naval bases (Guanaja and Caratasca) meant to strengthen the country's capacity to combat drug trafficking (Lindsay-Poland 2011). In Fiscal Year 2011, the Pentagon increased its contract spending in Honduras to $53.8 million, up 71 percent from the previous year (Lindsay-Poland 2012).

Additionally, the New York Times reported in May 2012 on new commando-style squads—called Foreign-deployed Advisory Support Teams or FAST—originally created by the Drug Enforcement Agency (DEA) in Afghanistan. With the wars in Iraq and Afghanistan winding down, FAST units have been brought to Honduras where they deploy from three so-called "forward operating bases" (Shanker 2012).[25] Along with the multi-million dollar expansion of Soto Cano, the infusion of resources in at least five Honduran bases since the coup amount to an "increasingly permanent US military presence in Honduras, now extending across all of the territory" (Honduras Culture and Politics 2011).[26]

That this military build-up is being carried out in the name of the War on Drugs raises serious concerns, especially considering recently released information linking the Honduran elite with drug trafficking. In a cable published by WikiLeaks, the US State Department admits having knowledge of a Cessna aircraft containing 1,400 kilos of cocaine found on Miguel Facussé's property (Frank 2011). Peasant workers speak (cautiously and anonymously) of secret landing strips located deep inside the vast palm plantations.

The Aguán agro-oligarchs ostensibly benefit from both sides of the War on Drugs. In the first instance, as the leaked cable suggests, they benefit from drug trafficking, accumulating narco-wealth that can presumably be laundered through their numerous agrifood enterprises. In the second instance, they benefit from an increasingly militarized state that, in keeping with the national security doctrine of the 1980s, continues to attack an imprecise "internal enemy," thus keeping the population (especially the rural population) in a constant state of terror.

5
THE WAR ON PEASANTS

The war isn't against drug trafficking. This is a war on peasants.
—Adelio Muñoz, Peasant Movement of Orica[27]

For the peasant movements of the Aguán, who have been organizing to recuperate their lands since the late nineties (see Part Three), the 2009 coup abruptly terminated much of the progress made over more than a decade of struggle. Pro-peasant legislation passed by Zelaya was quickly overturned after the coup while the militarization of the Aguán further reinforced the power of the agro-oligarchy.

Shortly before he was overthrown, Zelaya had agreed to grant land titles to peasants who had peacefully occupied and produced on their lands for ten years or more. Decree Law 18-2008 would have purportedly resolved an estimated 426 land conflicts (a collection of unresolved disputes known as the *mora agraria*), titling 40,000 hectares (over 98,000 acres) of land for the benefit of approximately 20,000 peasant families (Proceso Digital 2011). The law, passed by the National Congress under Zelaya in March 2009, was declared unconstitutional under Lobo in November 2010 after the large landowners' association, the National Federation of Farmers and Ranchers (FENAGH) argued that it "violated private property and free enterprise" (ibid.). Indeed, FENAGH had been campaigning to delegitimize Law 18-2008 since its passing, calling it an "expropriation decree" and claiming it would "scare away investors" (La Prensa 2008a).

In practice, the reversal of the law meant that any community without proof of legal title, no matter how long it had lived on the land, was vulnerable to eviction. Shortly after the decision, eighty Maya Chortí indigenous families of the ancient Copán ruins zone—an important development area for "cultural tourism"—were threatened by an investor who bought the land from under them. The National Agrarian Institute (INA) pledged 8 million lempiras (approximately US$400,000) to resolve the conflict by October of 2011, but the money never came. The community, which had farmed the land for over twenty years, was forcibly removed in mid-December of that year (El Heraldo 2011e).

The violence unleashed on pro-democracy protesters by coup leader Roberto Micheletti (June 2009 – January 2010) hit peasant communities especially hard. In the department of Colón, where the Aguán Valley is located, the nation-wide curfew had "extended hours" (beginning at 6pm in Colón and 10pm in most of the country) restricting the movement of peasants to and from their fields, and preventing them from engaging with the national anti-coup resistance (CEJIL 2009). Anyone found defying the 6pm curfew was subject to detention, and potentially torture or disappearance.

Under Lobo's government, which came to power in January 2010 through post-coup elections, the Aguán has been pummeled by repeated waves of state-sponsored violence including constant surveillance, death threats, capture orders, kidnappings, sexual violence, torture and assassinations. After the private guards of Miguel Facussé murdered five peasant members of MCA in November 2010—an event known as the Tumbador massacre—the military occupied the valley, including the offices of the National Agrarian Institute (INA), for two months (FIDH 2011, 14). Using the massacre as a pretext for militarization, the deployment was called "Operation Tumbador" (24).

For Daniel Gómez, a member of the Unified Movement of Aguán Peasants (MUCA), the motive of the coup is crystal clear:

Military presence in the community of Guadalupe Carney, Aguán (photo by Roger Harris)

"The coup wasn't against Mel Zelaya, it was against us. To silence our voices and our demands for land."[28]

The human rights organization COFADEH documented 4,234 human rights violations in the country in the three months following the coup—including extra-judicial killings, torture and illegal detentions—most of which have still not been properly investigated (COFADEH 2009). On top of this rampant impunity, high-ranking military officials linked to the coup were awarded public offices under the Lobo government,[29] including coup-leader Micheletti, who was given amnesty and (unconstitutionally) named "senator for life" (FIDH 2011, 7).

Since the coup, violence has escalated throughout the country. In the elite-controlled media, the violence is disconnected from the state and instead is blamed on street gangs and drug traffickers. Meyer (2011) notes:

> Many have assumed that gangs are responsible for the increasing number of homicides; however, recent studies have shown that the highest murder rates are not

in large cities—where gangs are primarily located—but in more remote areas along strategic drug trafficking corridors.

It just so happens that the "strategic drug trafficking corridors" are also the areas of major agribusiness and tourism expansion. Thus, the violence perpetrated by private guards, military and police against peasants on large palm plantations and coastal indigenous communities is easily recast as "drug-related" violence. Drug trafficking (and the purported presence of "foreign insurgents" from Nicaragua or Colombia) is then used as a justification for troop deployments in the region, with the end result of repressing peasant movements. The media reinforces this ideology of terror, routinely insinuating that peasant communities themselves are responsible for drug-related violence, thus justifying peasant repression.[30]

Seen in this light, the War on Drugs not only does little to curb drug trafficking; it actually props up those who reap its benefits, granting them a veil of impunity. It also creates a militarized climate that represses peasant movements, thus enabling the oligarchy to cement its control over the entire valley (indeed the entire northern coast). Between September 2009 and August 2012, there were 53 recorded peasant murders linked to the security forces of large oil palm growers (FIAN 2012; IACHR 2012). Many Aguán peasants and activists place the death toll at over 60 (Bird 2012). Officials have carried out evictions and other violent acts on behalf of large landowners, and private security personnel have been seen wearing borrowed military and police uniforms to carry out repression.[31] Since the coup, notes MUCA member Daniel Gómez, "it has become very dangerous to walk around wearing boots and a straw hat; it has become dangerous to look like a *campesino*."[32]

PART 2

PALM OIL AND THE CORPORATE FOOD REGIME

Palm oil proponents make a number of claims in defense of the industry: that it produces food for a growing global population; alleviates poverty through smallholder development and economic growth; and addresses climate change by efficiently producing green alternatives to fossil fuel (World Growth 2011; PalmOil HQ 2009). It is a narrative that casts palm oil in a rather heroic role: that of feeding the world, ending poverty and saving the planet—all while making astronomical profits—a win-win (-win) scenario.[33]

Part Two begins by addressing some of the underlying assumptions of these claims, arguing that the rapid expansion of oil palm has not been a natural response to global market forces, much less an altruistic project to feed the hungry. Rather, the global oil palm boom has been driven by huge public subsidies for the sector—such as multi-million dollar financing from the World Bank Group—combined with trade liberalization, investment deregulation and the privatization of land and other public resources. Together, these rules and policies govern how food is produced, processed, distributed and sold, and who controls these processes. McMichael (2004; 2009) uses the term "corporate food regime" to describe the complex set of rules—enforced by institutions like the World Bank, WTO and free trade agreements—that institutionalize corporate power in the food system from seed to table. As can be seen from the previous chapter, this regime is also backed by militarization, dispossession and the criminalization of resistance.

The last two chapters of Part Two concern the "greening" of the corporate food regime, a trend in which corporate actors legitimize and expand their hold on power by appealing to environmental concerns within the new green economy. In so doing, they can also exploit new market opportunities for "green" products, including renewable energy, ecotourism, carbon offsets and ecosystem services. The term "green grabbing" has been coined to describe this deeply troubling emerging trend, in which lands and resources used to sustain livelihoods are appropriated by capital in the name of the environment (Fairhead et al. 2012).

6
THE MAKING OF A "FOOD-LIKE SUBSTANCE"

It is expected that 45 out of every 100 additional calories in the period up to 2030 may come from oil crops. During the last 10 years, consumption of oils and fats has increased by 10 million tons…
Oil palm's contribution as a stabilizing crop to global food security is now undisputed.
—*Datuk Carl Bek-Nielsen, Executive Director of United Plantations, keynote speech at the 2012 Palm & Lauric Oils Conference, Kuala Lumpur, Malaysia*[34]

In its native West Africa, oil palm is traditionally cultivated by smallholders in wetland groves, intercropped with food staples like yam and cassava. Its oil is expelled using artisan methods and consumed as an ingredient in traditional dishes, palm wine and medicines. In the early twentieth century, however, companies like Lever Brothers (now Unilever) and United Fruit began investing in technologies to make oil palm a viable plantation crop and its oil suitable for export. Corporate agronomists developed new hybrids that responded well to the tropical soils of Southeast Asia and Latin America; and chemists developed new techniques to transform the oil into a clear, bland fat suitable for Western palates known as "refined, bleached and deodorized" or RBD palm oil (Kiple and Ornelas 2000). Red in color, unrefined palm oil is one of the richest sources of carotenoids in the world, but these nutrients are removed in its processing.

The majority of the world's palm oil is now transformed into what food writer Michael Pollan (2008) calls "edible food-like substances"—industrial food products low in nutritional value but high in calories from sugar and saturated fat.

Palm-derived food additives are now found in roughly half of the packaged foods in the modern supermarket, with ingredient names like palmitate, palmate, sodium lauryl sulphate, glyceryl stearate and stearic acid (Richardson 2011).[35] Or it may simply be listed as "vegetable oil." Palm oil is also used in the growing "oleochemicals" industry (See Box 3) to produce manufactured goods like soaps, lubricants, candles, detergents, cosmetics, pharmaceuticals and increasingly fuel (biodiesel). This rapid development of industrial uses for palm oil corresponds to an explosion in the area planted to oil palm. Between 1980 and 2009, the global area increased eightfold, from about 1.55 million hectares to 12.2 million hectares (about 30 million acres) primarily in the equatorial tropics (World Bank 2011). Malaysia and Indonesia are by far the world's largest producers, accounting for more than 85 percent of global production, with other significant producers in Africa, Asia and Latin America. The crop is now produced in large-scale industrial monocultures of uniform age structure, with sparse undergrowth and intensive use of fertilizers and pesticides (UNEP 2011).[36]

The increased availability and affordability of palm oil has led to a dramatic increase in its consumption, especially in the "emerging economies" of the Global South: rapidly industrializing G-20 countries such as China, India, Mexico, Brazil and South Korea. Linked to rising levels of obesity and diet-related disease, this trend has had devastating impacts on public health worldwide. Consumption of vegetable oil is the leading cause of what health experts call the "nutritional transition," a shift away from traditional diets rich in fiber and grain towards a diet high in animal products, oils and fats, refined sweeteners and processed carbohydrates (Popkin 1999; Hawkes 2006; Glodhaber-Fieber et al. 2011). While normally attributed primarily to the increased consumption of meat and dairy, the road

BOX 3. THE OLEOCHEMICALS INDUSTRY

Prior to 1980, palm oil was mainly refined and sold as edible oil (Appalasami and de Vries 1990). Corporate researchers are now hard at work developing expanded applications for palm oil (derived from palm fruit) and palm kernel oil (derived from the inner seed or kernel). Since the early eighties, there has been an increasing use of these oils as raw material for the production of "oleochemicals," chemical products derived from plant and animal fats such as palm, coconut, rapeseed (canola), soybean and tallow.

The oleochemicals industry emerged after a slump in the production of petrochemicals—chemicals derived from petroleum—due to the spike in crude oil prices in the 1970s (Haupt et al. 1984). Much like petrochemicals, oleochemicals are used in a variety of products: soaps and detergents; lubricants; coatings and resins; plastics; candles; paper; rubber; food and feed; tobacco products; polyurethanes; cosmetics; pharmaceuticals; emulsifiers and anti-static agents; and explosives (Rupilius and Ahmad 2005). These are produced from four basic groups of oleochemicals: fatty acids, fatty alcohols, glycerine and methyl esters.

In addition to the growing markets for edible oil and biodiesel, the oleochemicals industry represents practically limitless markets for palm oil expansion. Of course, while markets may be limitless, land and water resources are not. "Natural" limits notwithstanding, Appalasami and de Vries (1990) commented, "there are few, if any, applications, for which palm-derived oleochemicals cannot be used."

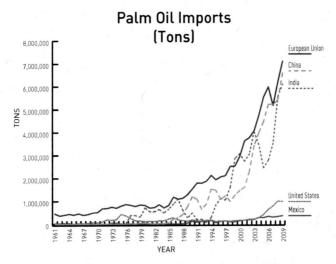

Chart 1. Palm Oil Imports. Chart constructed by the author with data from FAOstat.fao.org > Trade > Crops and Livestock Products (data retrieved May 5, 2012)

to Western-style over-consumption typically begins with major increases in domestic production and imports of refined vegetable oil (Chopra 2002).

Since the mid-1970s, Asia has replaced Europe as the biggest importer of palm oil, with China and India in the lead (Kongsager and Reenberg 2012). In India, trade liberalization in the 1990s led to a surge in soybean oil and palm oil imports. As a result, a recent study in the journal *Current Science* notes that Indian "oil consumption has surpassed all earlier predictions and may continue to increase at a blistering pace" (Sharma 2012). Per capita consumption of edible oils shot up from 3 kg per year in 1950 to 14.2 kg in 2011, leading to growing rates of cardiovascular problems in the country (ibid.). In China, per capita oil consumption reached 23 kg in 2009, more than double the recommended annual fat intake of 10.5 kg per year (ibid.).

While it may be true that the world is consuming more palm oil than ever before, this does not necessarily make it an *undisputed* contributor to global food security, as Bek-Nielsen, executive director of United Plantations (the 12th largest public palm oil company) would have it (Reuters 2008). First, palm oil does not necessarily cater to the world's hungriest people in the poorest countries, but rather to consumers primarily located in G-20 countries. Seventy-one percent of Honduran palm oil exports, for instance, are destined for Mexico where, like China and India, diets are rapidly industrializing (SAG 2009, 8). Second, palm oil consumption is linked to a deepening public health crisis, primarily among the urban poor. For populations separated from the land and the ability to grow food, and with limited income-earning opportunities, cheap calories may be a question of short-term survival. But this "consumer choice" is hardly a choice at all. It is a choice structured by poverty on one hand, and the power of food corporations on the other.

Third, corporate palm oil producers are increasingly adapting their production processes to respond to rapidly changing global market conditions. Borras et al. (2012) use the term "flex crops" to refer to crops that have many potential uses (e.g. food, feed, fuel, industrial material) and can thus be sold in whatever form fetches the highest market price—in other words, not necessarily as food for human consumption. And finally, those who reap the highest profits from palm oil production are generally the large processors and exporters, not rural communities. Thus, "it is not 'development' for producing regions so much as for investors" (McMichael 2012, 692). In fact, far from supporting food security, palm oil can generate rural hunger. One peasant worker and MUCA member comments:

> Since our lands were taken away, the money supply throughout the Aguán has decreased dramatically. People had to go work as laborers on plantations and never saw the growth they were promised. Unemployment and underemployment increased, as did hunger and despair. Now, workers don't even have enough money to buy food for the entire month. This kind of production generates wealth only for the large businessmen. (Trucchi 2010)

In a study of northern Guatemala, Alonso-Fradejas (2012) shows that "peasant-farmed crops/systems generate up to ten times more 'local wealth' per hectare than corporate sugarcane and oil palm" (10). As such, the region's economy benefits little, if at all, from the expansion of corporate plantations. In Honduras, where the expansion of oil palm has come primarily at the expense of subsistence food production and the peasant economy in the Aguán, "food security" is a feeble justification indeed for continued corporate expansion in the oil palm sector.

7

SUBSIDIZING CORPORATE EXPANSION

Despite its many negative impacts, oil palm continues to expand due to the high profits to be gained in the sector. The crop's short growth cycle, low production costs (thanks in part to land and resource grabs), lack of environmental controls, expanding consumer market and easy availability of financing all contribute to the sector's profitability (Carrere 2006). For countries struggling to service high external debts, the export-oriented crop is a particularly attractive means of generating foreign exchange. Since the 1960s, aid from institutions like the World Bank Group and the Inter-American Development Bank Group (IDB) has served as a large subsidy to the oil palm industry, first building up the required public infrastructure, and later investing heavily in private companies.

Since 1965, the World Bank (IBRD/IDA) has committed US$2 billion to 45 palm oil projects, a third of which went to Indonesia (IFC 2011, 55). Most of the projects were implemented in the public sector in the 1970s. These were of a more classic "development" orientation, focused on building state capacity through the construction of processing plants, mills, roads, extension services and credit facilities to develop smallholder farms and in some cases outgrower schemes (contract farming). But when public sector financing for agriculture decreased to a trickle in the 1980s and 90s, the Bank's *private sector* lending arm, the International Finance Corporation (IFC), began ramping up investments to agro-export projects like palm oil. IFC funding targeted much larger operations and moved down into the palm oil supply chain, with substantial investments in trading, refining and manufacturing (Hai Teoh 2011).

These large investments in the corporate sector, combined with the volatility of the global market, favor "economies of scale" that put smallholders at a severe disadvantage. When increased supply depresses international palm oil prices—as it did following the 2008 price spike—large-scale producers benefit. Lower prices for palm oil make it more competitive in the global market vis-à-vis other oils like soybean and rapeseed (canola). With lower production costs and higher volume, large producers are able to compete. Small and medium producers, however, are caught in the infamous "cost-price squeeze."

Coupled with trade liberalization, smallholders cannot hope to compete. In late 2008 and 2009, around 4,500 peasant oil palm producers in northern Honduras found themselves on the brink of bankruptcy due to rising input costs and the falling price received for palm fruit (La Prensa 2008c; El Heraldo 2009b).

Of course, there is nothing new about this strategy: large-scale producers capture subsidies, over-produce and drive down world prices, thus ruining smallholders while at the same time stimulating global consumption. The same is true of any commodity, whether it be wheat, bananas or cotton.[37]

Thanks to SAPs and the influx of investment, the area dedicated to oil palm in Honduras has increased dramatically, from around 40,000 hectares in 1990 to 82,100 hectares in 2005 to 120,000 hectares in 2009 (SAG 2009). Honduras currently produces more than 300,000 tons of palm oil, 70 percent of which is exported, primarily to Mexico (FIDH 2011, 8).[38] And while Honduran agriculture suffered a steep overall decline in the 1990s, the oil palm sector jumped from 3.2 percent of the GDP in 1992 to 10 percent in 2003 (Sanders et al. 2006). The benefits of this growth have been concentrated in the hands of a few powerful, Honduran-based agro-food corporations.

Miguel Facussé's vertically-integrated operations—producing

Aerial view of oil palm plantations in Malaysia (photo by Wakx/Creative Commons)

palm, edible oil, snack foods, manufactured goods and a small amount of biodiesel—have been the main beneficiaries of IFC palm sector investments in Honduras. Facussé's Cressida Corporation received $55 million in 1997 and his Dinant Corporation received $30 million in 2008 for the expansion of production, manufacturing and distribution of palm oil products (IFC 1997; 2009a).[39] Dinant also received $7 million in 2009 from the Inter-American Investment Corporation (IIC), the private sector lending arm of the IDB, which stated, "It is important for leading companies such as Grupo Dinant to continue to grow and invest in the region" (IFC 2009a). Both Cressida and Dinant are responsible for grabbing large tracts of Aguán lands in the early nineties. There is also a proposed $25 million IFC investment to René Morales Carazo's Grupo Jaremar, another agro-foods giant linked to land grabs and repression in the Aguán (IFC 2009b).

These large capital investments may not be *directly* responsible for land grabs in the Aguán, but they play an important role in facilitating them. Economies of scale demand that an oil palm plantation be at least 4,000 hectares (9,884 acres) in size in order to feasibly operate a crude palm oil mill (World Rainforest Movement 2006). In Southeast Asia, the "sourcing area" for a typical palm oil mill averages around 10,000 hectares (24,710 acres) from a combination of large processor-owned plantations and small independent farms locked into production contracts (Deininger and Byerlee 2011). Honduran mills serve 7,000 to 10,000 hectares on average (Defontenay 1999). This means that investments in increased milling and processing capacity—though not directly involved in land acquisition—are likely to promote the expansion of oil palm production onto new lands. As Borras et al. (2012) argue, "in some settings, even more important than the *scale of land acquisitions* is the *scale of capital* involved" (856).

With this kind of investment, and the possibility for high returns, it is no wonder oil palm can be found in the investment portfolios of an increasing number of transnational agro-food corporations. According to the 2009 World Investment Report, eight of the world's 25 largest agriculture-based companies have major interests in oil palm (cited in Deininger and Byerlee 2011, 7). The trend of oil palm expansion, as well as corporate concentration, is driven in part by large public subsidies from institutions like the World Bank Group and IDB for "economies of scale" in the palm oil sector.

8
FREE TRADE AND FAST FOOD

The expansion of oil palm and other export-oriented activities like logging and ranching have come at the expense of food crops such as corn, beans, rice and sorghum, which were either eliminated or pushed onto poor soils and steep hillsides. This process has been accompanied by a transformation of local diets, marked by an increased presence of imported and processed foods, and a surge in American fast food outlets.

The number of chain restaurants in Honduras exploded in the 1990s after the first such outlet—a Burger King franchise—was offered tax-exempt status under the pretext of promoting tourism. The tax loophole was expanded with the passage of the 1998 Tourism Promotion Law, which granted ten-year tax holidays for "tourism-related businesses," including hotels, resorts and fast food restaurants (US Embassy 2004). Much like the concentration of land ownership, the concentration of power in the food industry soared in the 1990s. A US embassy cable (released by WikiLeaks) from the eve of the country's first Quiznos restaurant opening in 2004 explains:

> Though there are myriad US franchised fast-food
> operations in Honduras already, most are owned by
> only a handful of firms or families. Eduardo Kafati, for
> example, holds franchise rights to Burger King, Church's
> Chicken, Popeye's Chicken and Biscuits, Little Ceasars

Pizza, Baskin-Robbins, and Dunkin Donuts. Similarly, Roberto Larach (publisher of two major newspapers and a cousin of the Canahuati family) holds the rights to Pizza Hut, Kentucky Fried Chicken, and the Pepsi distributorship in San Pedro. Wendy's Hamburgers and casual dining restaurant Applebee's are owned by shopping-mall magnate Raymond Malouf. (…) The [Quiznos-owning] Rock family is a new entry to this sector, but is not without other connections: Antonio Rock is brother-in-law to the powerful Canahuati clan, the family of Ambassador to the US Mario Canahuati and owners of a multi-million dollar maquila operation. (ibid.)

Along with the landowning elite, these highly influential corporate food families (Kafati, Larach, Canahuati), with strong ties to US capital, are widely known to have supported the 2009 coup (Méndez 2009; Paley 2010). Honduras thus offers a striking example of how an undemocratic food system mirrors and upholds an undemocratic political system.

US fast food chains in Tegucigalpa (photo by T. Kerssen)

CAFTA-DR, often referred to simply as CAFTA, further facilitated the expansion of transnational food corporations, creating major changes regarding what food is available to consumers throughout Central America. Under CAFTA, approximately 80 percent of US industrial and consumer goods, and over 50 percent of US agricultural exports, now enter Central America duty-free. Tariffs for nearly all remaining products will be eliminated by 2020 (USTR 2009). According to the US Commercial Service's "Doing Business in Honduras" guide, US exporters "enjoy an enviable position in the Honduran market [which] has improved after the implementation of CAFTA" (US Commercial Service 2011). Lobo's Investment Protection and Promotion Law (2011) further deepened CAFTA's free trade commitments, setting the bar extremely low for market entry.[40]

Following the coup, US aid provided further incentives for investment in the Honduran food system. The Obama administration's Feed the Future initiative, administered by USAID, opened the door to greater corporate control over agricultural supply chains (See Box 4).

According to the USDA Foreign Agricultural Service's "Exporter's Guide" Honduras now has the largest number of fast food franchises in Central America and a rapidly expanding supermarket sector (USDA-FAS 2012a). At the time of this writing, the construction of the "biggest shopping mall in Central America" (131,000 square meters) is nearing completion in Tegucigalpa (El Heraldo 2011a). With various new projects in the works—from luxury resorts and cruise ship docks to gated communities and apartment-hotels—tourism also plays a significant role in stimulating North American investments and imports. These factors create enticing markets for US exporters of agricultural commodities (e.g. wheat, rice and beef); processed foods (canned fruits and vegetables); consumer products (snacks and condiments); and food processing and packaging equipment (USDA-FAS 2012a). In other words, the industrialization of consumption is generating new profit-making opportunities for foreign companies—much like the industrialization of

BOX 4. USAID'S "FEED THE FUTURE" INITIATIVE

In Honduras, the global food crisis of 2008 was exacerbated by the June 2009 coup, worsening food and fuel prices and freezing many public services (Juventud Rebelde 2009). In view of the need to legitimize an unpopular government amidst a twin food and political crisis, the Obama administration selected Honduras as one of twenty "focus countries" for its new Feed the Future (FTF) initiative. FTF assistance to Honduras (over $30 million in its first two years) named food security as a "fundamental piece of the Embassy Country Team's response to the crisis" (FTF 2011).

Under the coordination of USAID, FTF's approach echoes the view of the dominant aid institutions (and USAID's earlier influence on SAPs) about the inefficiency of peasant food producers. The first FTF implementation report for Honduras states, "many households in rural hillside areas seem to be locked into a vicious cycle of producing basic grains, mainly for subsistence consumption (...) blocking the transition to other income-earning strategies that would possibly be more profitable" (FTF 2010). But one must ask, more profitable for whom?

Rather than help farmers access the land and resources needed to produce food sustainably for local markets, FTF integrates smallholders into export horticulture projects through its core program, ACCESSO.[41] As is standard practice for USAID, the program is managed by an American private contractor (Fintrac, Inc.). Towards meeting its goal of "creating economies of scale" the program joined forces with Wal-Mart. The new FTF-Wal-Mart-USAID partnership aims to incorporate Central American farmers into the mega-retailer's supply chain and develop their ability to meet corporate standards (USAID 2011a). Signed in March 2011, the agreement dovetailed with Wal-Mart's aggressive expansion plan into Central America. Wal-Mex, the store's Mexico and Central America division, opened 373 new retail outlets in 2011, bringing the total number of stores in the region up to 2,655 (Terra 2011).

Wal-Mart's move southward is tied to the rural crisis and the flow of migrants northward. Rocha (2011) argues that remittances from the US give families remaining in Central America just enough disposable income to be seen as a profitable consumer market for the retail giant. In addition, FTF gives Wal-Mart greater control over how and what small farmers produce.[42] The Wal-Mart boom is part of the broader corporatization of consumption in Honduras and Central America, facilitated by US-backed trade and aid policies (CAFTA, FTF).

Tegucigalpa graffiti reads "Burger Golpista (coup supporter)" (photo by T. Kerssen)

agriculture generates new profits for seed, energy and chemical companies. Indeed, these are two sides of the same coin: a food system controlled increasingly by global monopoly capital.

Honduras also has bilateral free trade agreements with Mexico, Colombia, Panama, Chile, Taiwan and most recently Canada. The country also signed (along with Costa Rica, El Salvador, Guatemala, Nicaragua and Panama) a comprehensive trade agreement with the European Union on June 29, 2012 (SICE 2012). But as Honduras' chief trading partner (supplying 50.1 percent of imports and purchasing 59.5 percent of exports in 2009), the United States remains the most influential player (US Commercial Service 2011). With Central America's largest deep-water port, Puerto Cortés, Honduras also serves as a distribution platform for the entire region. This makes Honduras a strategic "gateway" for corporate food in Central America and the Caribbean.

9
GREENING THE REGIME, PART 1: FUELING THE GREEN ECONOMY

Palm oil isn't just wonderful for your health when used for frying; it could also be a great substitute for petroleum, which is becoming scarcer and more expensive.
– Miguel Facussé, quoted in El Heraldo, *April 2011*

In addition to feeding a growing global appetite for vegetable oil and processed food, palm oil is also seen as a promising feedstock for the production of liquid biofuel, also known as "agrofuels." Along with a growing number of markets for "green" products, agrofuels can provide a cloak of legitimacy for corporate land grabbing. "Green grabbing" occurs when land and resources are appropriated—with local land users often expelled—in the name of producing renewable fuel, sequestering carbon, promoting ecotourism or other "environmental" pursuits (Fairhead et al. 2012). This chapter explores the growing market for palm-based fuel, and the emerging set of global mechanisms that allow corporations to capture value in the green economy. At the same time, these mechanisms dangerously re-cast the palm oil oligarchy as saviors of the environment.

Since the late 1990s there has been a strong interest in ethanol (primarily from maize and sugarcane) and biodiesel (from oil crops like soy, rapeseed, palm oil and jatropha) as an alternative or supplement to costly fossil fuels. For the newly consolidated agro-oligarchies of the Global South—where the agrofuels

expansion is primarily occurring—agrofuels represent an enticing new opportunity for accumulation, global integration and
"green" credentials.

While the majority of the world's palm oil is currently destined for human consumption, the use of palm oil for energy is
expected to increase due to rising energy prices as well as government targets, international aid and other subsidies that increase
demand.[43] The main drivers of the global agrofuels market are
the European Union and the United States. The US National
Academy of Sciences found, for instance, that even if all the corn
and soybeans produced in the US in 2005 were used for fuel,
this would only have met 12 percent of the country's gasoline
demand and 6 percent of its diesel demand (cited in Eide 2009).
Likewise, 47 percent of EU oilseed production currently goes to
biodiesel, serving only a tiny percentage of European fuel needs
(ibid.). The diversion of Northern-produced oil crops such as soy
and rapeseed towards fuel uses increases the demand for palm oil
in food. The surge of palm oil in European diets is due to the
diversion of half of the annual European rapeseed harvest toward
biodiesel (Kongsager and Reenberg 2012).

Any major increase in the US and European consumption
of agrofuels will have to be met by production increases in the
Global South. The EU's renewable fuel targets, for instance,
require that 10 percent of transport fuels be supplied by renew-
ables by 2020. It is expected that 80 to 90 percent of this target
will be met by imported agrofuels, mainly palm oil (Anseeuw et
al. 2012). According to a recent FAO report (Eide 2009), government targets in the North have unleashed a veritable "biofuel
fever" in the global South. The research group GRAIN (2007)
reported that agrofuel investments in Malaysia and Singapore
had reached "frenzied levels."

In Honduras, the "Law for the Production and Consumption
of Biofuels" passed in November 2007 provides exemptions
from customs tariffs, income tax, and other related taxes for biofuel companies for twelve years (USDA-FAS 2010). The same
year, a $7 million loan from the Central American Bank of

Economic Integration (CABEI) was used to import over one million improved oil palm seedlings from Malaysia, enough to plant over 7,000 additional hectares (ibid.).[44]

Of eleven palm oil processing plants in Honduras,[45] five have the capacity to produce palm oil biodiesel, known as palm methyl ester, or PME. The two plants with the largest capacity are Miguel Facussé's Dinant plant and René Morales Carazo's Jaremar plant, followed by three much smaller peasant-owned plants[46] (See Chart 2). Due to the high global demand for palm oil in food and the high cost of processing it into PME, none of these plants currently produce biodiesel for export. Dinant and Jaremar produce small amounts for use by company vehicles and machinery (USDA-FAS 2010; IICA 2010).

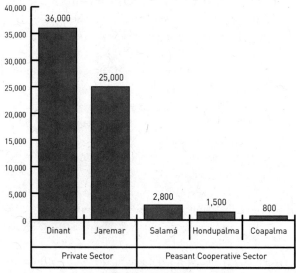

Chart 2. Installed Capacity to Produce Biodiesel. Chart constructed by the author with data from PRONAGRO, Ministry of Agriculture and Livestock (cited in USDA-FAS 2010)

Dinant and Jaremar are clearly the best situated to take advantage of export markets for agrofuels as demand increases, especially in Europe. Their market position is further strengthened by bilateral and multilateral aid flows supporting economies of scale at the expense of the peasant sector. Roberto Vellutini, head of private sector lending for Energy and Infrastructure at the IDB (one of the biggest promoters of agrofuels in Latin America), commented:

> Tropical countries have optimum conditions for producing biofuels at lower cost, so it makes sense for multinationals in both agriculture and energy to invest in Brazil and other countries in Latin America, Africa and Asia. This will also lead to consolidation, as small-scale farming operations, cooperatives and family-owned businesses either merge or are purchased by larger companies. (Constance 2008)

The sanitized language of "mergers" and "consolidation" here masks the violence of land grabs; the creation of new droves of landless poor; and the bloody land and resource conflicts that result.

While the United States does not currently use PME as a renewable blending fuel, US officials and corporations have shown interest in Honduran agrofuels, especially since the 2009 coup. WikiLeaks revealed that congressman Dana Rohrabacher (R-California) traveled to Honduras in December 2009, before the Lobo government was recognized by the US, accompanied by real estate investors and top executives from the company SG Biofuels, a San Diego-based firm specializing in the oilseed crop jatropha (Lipton 2010).[47] In meetings with Lobo and other government officials, Rohrabacher praised the ouster of president Zelaya and "enthusiastically promoted the biofuel company's plans to set up operations in Honduras" (ibid.).

In April 2011, president Obama nominated Lisa Kubiske as the new US ambassador to Honduras—a diplomat with strong credentials brokering US-Brazilian biofuels cooperation—sending a clear message that the US government intends to facilitate US corporate interests in Honduran agrofuels (Bird 2011). In addition to palm oil, jatropha and tilapia oil are viewed as the most promising renewable energy sources to develop in Honduras (IICA 2010).

Another factor promoting the expansion of oil palm is the new global market in Certified Emission Reduction credits (CERs), also known as carbon credits, through the UN's Clean Development Mechanism (CDM), a climate change mitigation program initiated under the Kyoto Protocol. CERs—each one equivalent to one ton of carbon dioxide (CO_2)—are awarded to projects in the developing world that reduce the amount of greenhouse gases released into the atmosphere. CERs can then be sold to polluters in industrialized countries to help meet emission reduction commitments under Kyoto. These credits are not necessarily granted for the production of PME, which has one of the lowest emission reduction values of any source

AGROPALMA (Jaremar) palm oil processing plant in the Aguán, owned by large landowner René Morales (photo by T. Kerssen)

of biofuel, largely because of its contribution to deforestation in Southeast Asia.[48] Nonetheless, CERs are increasingly granted for the creation of facilities that generate energy from the waste products of palm oil production.

Palm oil manufacturing is a highly polluting industry, generating three main kinds of waste: solid waste (fibers, shells and empty fruit bunches); liquid waste (generated in the oil extraction process); and air emissions (smoke from boilers and incinerators). The combination of liquid waste with cooling water generates what is known as palm oil mill effluent (POME), a substance that may be dumped in nearby waterways, killing marine life and contaminating the water for drinking and bathing (CSPI 2005, 23). Alternatively, POME is stored in open lagoons, generating a biogas that contains about 65 percent methane (CH_4), one of the most potent greenhouse gases (Panapanaan et al. 2009). The incineration of empty fruit bunches (EFBs) also emits particulates into the atmosphere, and the indiscriminate dumping of EFBs causes additional methane emissions, as the plant matter decomposes.

Most of the palm-related CER projects are characterized as "methane mitigation" or "methane avoidance" projects, since they capture methane from wastewater that would otherwise be emitted or avoid methane emissions from the decay of biomass by using it as a fuel source instead. The reduction in greenhouse gas emissions is determined using a hypothetical "baseline scenario" characterized by business-as-usual practices (namely, the dumping of EFBs and the storage of POME in open lagoons). As the advocacy group GAIA (n.d.) points out, CERs offer "no incentive for choosing the best policy option." A palm oil mill processing thousands of hectares worth of palm fruit might receive CERs to reduce its emissions, while alternative rural development approaches (such as agrarian reform and diversified food production) would never even be considered.

In July 2011, amidst international outcry, the Executive Board of the CDM approved a methane mitigation project run by Exportadora del Atlántico as a recipient of carbon credits in the amount of approximately US$3.6 million (Eco2data 2012). Exportadora del Atlántico is a subsidiary of Dinant, owned by Miguel Facussé. According to watchdog group Biofuel-Watch, CDM's decision will "almost certainly allow Grupo Dinant to have their palm oil classed as a 'sustainable' EU biofuel feedstock" (Biofuel-Watch 2011). This is because in order to qualify for use as a "renewable fuel" in the EU market, a biofuel source must reduce emissions by at least 35 percent compared to fossil fuels. Without methane mitigation, PME is calculated at only 19 percent, disqualifying it as a blending fuel. With methane mitigation, the emission reduction value of PME increases to 56 percent (Pehnelt and Vietze 2010).

The CDM approval came after a German investment firm (DEG) and a French utility company (EDF) both withdrew from the project citing human rights concerns, following the release of a report documenting 23 peasant murders linked to Dinant (FIAN et al. 2011). In response to a letter signed by 70 human rights organizations denouncing the approval, CDM's European chairman Martin Hession from the UK responded that the board was simply "not equipped" to investigate human rights abuses (Biofuel-Watch 2010).

The CDM decision followed the signing of a Memorandum of Understanding between Miguel Facussé and World Wildlife Fund (WWF) in April 2010 endorsing Dinant's certification by the Roundtable on Sustainable Palm Oil (RSPO) (See Box 5). WWF has worked with a number of agribusinesses on the Caribbean coast of Central America, including Chiquita and Dole fruit companies, to reduce agrochemical runoff that threatens the Mesoamerican Reef, the second largest barrier reef in the world (WWF 2007). But WWF—like other Big Conservation groups such as Conservation International and the Nature Conservancy—has been strongly criticized for its cozy relationship with (and funding from) the world's biggest polluters (Rulli 2009; Hari 2010). Whether or not such arrangements lead to "impact reduction," they undoubtedly grant polluting corporations a sheen of environmental credibility.

BOX 5. THE ROUNDTABLE ON SUSTAINABLE PALM OIL

by Annie Shattuck[49]

The Roundtable on Sustainable Palm Oil (RSPO), the World Wildlife Fund's (WWF) first industry roundtable, has been in operation since 2002. Some of the largest players in the palm industry have been involved from the beginning. Groups like Cadbury Schweppes, Rabobank, and Wilmar International, a partially owned subsidiary of Unilever (whose Director of Sustainable Agriculture is president of the RSPO), have committed to the group's standards—which include respect for land rights, fair labor conditions and an end to deforestation. The RSPO includes an NGO-led "smallholder taskforce" to help smallholders participate in the certified market, and two locally based NGOs that help bring the voices of small farmers and indigenous people to the table.

Thus far, the Roundtable has not been able to significantly curb land conflicts or deforestation. In August of 2008, United Plantations was the first company to be certified under RSPO standards. According to the standards, a company plantation can be certified only if all their holdings meet certain minimum requirements; including no land conflicts, un-mediated labor disputes, or replacement of primary forest, and a plan to achieve certification for all plantations. According to Greenpeace, while the company's Malaysian plantation was certified, its holdings in Indonesia failed to comply with the RSPO's minimum standards for partial certification. Four community members were jailed for protesting oil palm development on their land in the Indonesian village of Rutu. One of the arrestees was still in prison when United Plantations converted the man's farm to oil palm. Furthermore, the Indonesian plantations were planted in "High Conservation Value Areas," on drained peatlands and recently cleared forests, prompting Greenpeace to call the RSPO's first test case a "failure."

While some civil society groups are calling on companies in the RSPO to live up to their promises of sustainability, others are calling the group's efforts "greenwashing" and claim the "RSPO is designed to legitimate the continuous expansion of the palm oil industry."

The WWF agreement with Facussé was signed in the midst of the first wave of heavy militarization in the Aguán, during a period of tense negotiations between the Lobo government, Facussé and MUCA. Over the course of these negotiations, eight Aguán peasants were murdered, six of whom were members of MUCA (FIDH 2011). The agreement with WWF allowed the company to downplay its role in this bloodbath over contested plantation lands, and highlight instead its commitment to sustainability. Facussé remarked:

> Our world is increasingly affected by pollution, habitat loss and the mismanagement of water resources. Transnational companies have woken up to the need to invest the best agricultural practices in order to guarantee the protection of areas like the Mesoamerican Reef. This is why by 2015, the largest buyers in the world will require that palm oil be certified by the Roundtable on Sustainable Palm Oil. With the support of WWF, the Dinant Corporation is implementing best practices to show the world that oil palm can be produced in a sustainable way, using modern science and technology. We are pioneers in conserving wildlife side by side with the development of industry, producing oil palm while maintaining biodiversity and reducing our environmental impact... By signing this MOU [with

WWF] we position our palm oil at the highest level of competitiveness with the biggest environmentally responsible producers in the world. I'm certain that this alliance will lead to our certification by the RSPO since WWF will attest to our commitment to the environment. We are entering this arena forcefully... it is necessary for our future, for our children and our grandchildren—of which I have many—in order to save the planet. (quoted in Nuila Coto 2010, author's translation)

Due to heavy criticism from grassroots and international human rights organizations, WWF temporarily suspended its work with Dinant in December 2010 "pending further investigation."[50]

Seeking to have the biggest impact, climate funding and certification schemes logically target the biggest operations. These are, in many cases, mega corporations like Honduras-based Dinant and Jaremar, or transnationals Cargill and Miller Brewing Company (all of which have received CERs for projects in Honduras).[51] Through CERs, they gain access to a whole new line of credit to modernize and expand production. They also gain a ready-made way to green their image and access new markets, e.g. for biodiesel or carbon offsets.[52]

In the case of the Aguán, the influence of climate funding mechanisms, green certification schemes (RSPO) and other manifestations of "green capitalism" are far from neutral. Rather, they further shift the balance of power in favor of large corporations and legitimize their activities on lands that were acquired through illegitimate or highly contested means. These new mechanisms facilitate "green grabbing"—the corporate takeover of land and resources in the name of the environment (Fairhead et al. 2012). In so doing, they also legitimize the violence used to repress or expel peasant and indigenous communities.

10

GREENING THE REGIME, PART 2: ECOTOURISM OR ECO-COLONIALISM?

Just when you thought you had everything…
—Advertisement for Njoi Beachfront Residences, Trujillo, Honduras[53]

A stone's throw away from the Aguán Valley is the spectacular Caribbean coast, a place of great natural beauty that has also become, like the Aguán, a key battleground in the struggle against corporate control of food, land and resources. Along with the expansion of agribusiness (oil palm, sugarcane, tropical fruit) and industrial zones (maquilas), the rapidly expanding coastal tourism complex is part of the broad corporate restructuring of northern Honduras.[54] This chapter looks at tourism developments in the region, which have facilitated land and resource grabs, primarily in Afro-indigenous Garifuna communities. Once again, "green" arguments—tied to the conservation of (estheticized) nature for tourism purposes—are used to advance a project of corporate control.[55]

Like Aguán peasants, Garifunas are engaged in an historic struggle for land, territory and control over their local economy. A unique Afro-Caribbean ethnic group, the Garifuna people are African descendants who escaped slavery in the Caribbean and intermixed with Amerindians (Caribs and Arawaks). Having evaded enslavement, they fought off the French and then the

British on the island of Saint Vincent before being deported to the island of Roatán off the coast of Honduras in 1796. Finding the island too small for their growing population, they appealed to the Spanish, who agreed to let them settle the isthmian mainland. From there, the Garifuna established settlements all along the Caribbean coast, maintaining their distinct language and culture, based primarily in fishing, hunting, small commerce and the cultivation of yuca, beans, bananas and coconut palm. Honduras has Central America's largest Garifuna population, with approximately 250,000 people in 48 coastal and island communities (Brondo and Brown 2011).

The Garifuna have inhabited the region for 215 years on lands they consider to be their ancestral territories. Indeed, they are considered a "tribal people" with the same rights as indigenous peoples by international bodies like the International Labor Organization (ILO) and the Inter-American Commission on Human Rights (IACHR 2010-2011, 282, n.72).[56] Garifuna communities maintained their territories through customary tenure (without formal land titles) until the 1990s, when land titling programs were

Garifuna woman with a conch shell horn at a protest march on the second anniversary of the coup, June 2011 (photo by Roger Harris)

instituted with funding from the World Bank.[57] Ironically, this is also when their lands came under the greatest threat.

In the early 1990s, at the height of structural adjustment, Central American governments began promoting tourism as a strategy to attract investment and donor funds. In Honduras, a presidential decree passed in August 1990 (Decree Law 90-90) weakened (some say violated) Article 107 of the national constitution prohibiting foreign property ownership within 40 kilometers (25 miles) of the coast. While the law did not amend the constitution, it made an "exception" to this prohibition for lands zoned as "urban" or lands with "tourism potential" (Brondo and Woods 2007; Ávila 2006; Meritas 2010).[58] This and other laws favoring tourism investments led to a rapid influx of investors to the isolated northern coast, previously an enclave economy dominated by North American fruit companies. Local elites also began enclosing properties to build vacation homes or rentals for tourists and visiting researchers.

In 1992, the Marbella Tourist Corporation began usurping property in the Garifuna community of Triunfo de la Cruz on Tela Bay, the largest Garifuna settlement in Honduras with 9,000 community members. When local residents formed the Committee to Defend the Land of Triunfo (CODETT), they began receiving threats from authorities. In 1997, three community leaders were murdered and a prominent anti-Marbella activist, Alfredo López, was arrested on trumped up drug trafficking charges. López spent seven years in jail until the Inter-American Court ruled in his favor and forced his release (Ryan 2008). Describing the ongoing assault on Garifuna communities, López comments, "We find ourselves in what can only be conceived as a war-like situation" (Rodríguez 2008). During the same period, oil palm plantations began encroaching on Triunfo and the greater Tela area, taking over communal lands previously used for growing and harvesting food (Guity 2009, 251).

The 1990s saw the emergence of an international "eco-development" agenda, using environmental language to promote large, multi-nodal conservation projects such as the Mesoamerican

Biological Corridor (MBC). Linked to other regional initiatives (CAFTA; Plan Puebla Panama), the MBC brought together national governments, international lenders, large conservation NGOs and the private sector under a rubric of "market-oriented conservation" (Finley-Brook 2007, 110). In practice, this usually meant opening up (and "securing") natural areas for extractive industries or tourism, under the watchful management of donor-funded NGOs (e.g. WWF, Conservation International, the Nature Conservancy) to ensure "sustainable" use.[59]

As part of this push, new marine reserves were created to protect aquatic resources (fish populations and coral reefs), designed to preserve the appeal of Honduran waters as a popular scuba diving destination (Moreno 2005, 222). The 1993 presidential decree creating the Cayos Cochinos Biological Reserve, for instance, included a moratorium on the removal of any marine life in the area. The decree thus prohibited fishing, collecting conch and diving for lobsters or other marine species—activities at the heart of Garifuna food culture and livelihoods (Brondo and Woods 2007). These prohibitions were enacted despite evidence that fish stock reduction is primarily caused not by artisanal fishers, but by the increased presence of industrial fishing fleets (Ryan 2008; FAO 2012). A Garifuna fisher from the community of Chachahuate commented:

> I understand that lobster is prohibited, but they must realize that we need it to feed our kids. If they catch us, they take our boats and kit. If one of our community members gets ill, we will catch lobster to pay for help on the mainland. That is life… One part of the management is being protective of the resources, and I believe our way of fishing does that. We use natural ways of fishing, using nets and minimal engine use. So our methods are fine for the environment. It is the big boats that come in bringing 3,000 lobster trays per boat, whereas our community doesn't even use 1,000 in the whole season. (Brondo and Brown 2011)

Restrictions also prohibited Garifunas from cutting down any trees or palms to build or repair their homes (Brondo and Woods 2007). As subsistence activities were increasingly criminalized, "a system of surveillance and policing was established, and navy patrols began to enforce the regulations" (7). Militarized conditions along the northern coast, including new US Navy installations on the island of Guanaja, have intensified the climate of repression, functioning to secure the neoliberal conservation/tourist complex against an increasingly marginalized local population.

While restrictions on Garifuna livelihood activities are ostensibly meant to protect aquatic resources for their long-term (i.e. sustainable) use by the elite-controlled tourism industry, the largely unregulated tourism boom has itself caused extensive damage:

> Many of the new roads on the islands are unstable and promote widespread erosion, siltation of offshore corals, and deterioration of streambeds and watersheds. Shoreline construction of hotels, restaurants, marinas, beaches, and housing has destroyed mangroves and corals. Hundreds of wells have been dug indiscriminately, leading to saltwater infiltration of the groundwater, disruption of groundwater flows and diminished stream quality. (Moreno 2005, 222)

From 1990 to 2000, the number of tourists visiting the Bay Islands increased from less than 10,000 annually to over 90,000 (ibid.). The increased number of scuba divers has damaged reefs and affected populations of juvenile fish, leading to resentment from (formerly) fishing-dependent communities (Brondo and Woods 2007, 12). This degradation also left Garifuna communities highly vulnerable to climate change and natural disasters such as Hurricane Mitch in 1998, which led to widespread coastal devastation. Crisis conditions after the storm were used as a pretext for promoting further growth in the corporate tourism sector (see Box 2).

Garifuna people argue that, far from being the cause of degradation, community control is the key to preserving watersheds,
biodiversity and fish populations, since their livelihoods depend
on the integrity of these resources. The Garifuna organization,
Black Fraternal Organization of Honduras (OFRANEH), which
has been struggling for decades against predatory tourism development, said in a statement:

> The northern coast of Honduras is considered one of the
> most vulnerable places in the world to climate change,
> and there is no doubt that this vulnerability is due to
> the unsustainable development practices of colonial
> powers. Coastal erosion devours our beaches at a rapid
> pace while prominent tourism investors appropriate the
> natural areas, which have been carefully conserved by
> our people and sustainably managed for our subsistence.
> (OFRANEH 2010a, author's translation)

After initial assaults on their lands by outside investors,
Garifuna organizations ramped up demands for territorial recognition from the state. In response, the National Agrarian Institute
(INA) implemented a program to deliver land titles to all 48
Garifuna communities, most of which were issued between
1993 and 2002 (Brondo and Brown 2011).[60] But the "agrarian reform" vision of the Honduran government and its funders
clashed with that of the Garifuna people. As Anderson (2007)
points out, multilateral institutions (in particular the World
Bank) promote territorial recognition "under the logic that a
secure property regime will create a viable climate for property
transfer and investment" (399). For Garifunas, land titles, whether
individual or communal, should serve the function of preserving
territorial and cultural integrity; i.e. they should *prevent* property
transfer and *protect* the community from outside investments that
are at odds with local needs.

Organizations like OFRANEH have critiqued titling programs
as inadequate for protecting their communities from land and

resource grabs, environmental degradation and other threats that undermine the reproduction of Garifuna culture. As both a critique and political demand, they invoke the concept of "functional habitat." In its most limited definition, functional habitat refers to community lands *plus* the surrounding lands, rivers, wilderness and marine areas upon which communities depend *even though they may not have direct ownership of them*. In its broadest sense, the concept refers to a territorial space that includes multiple communities, cultural interactions and relations of production and exchange (CCARC 2002; Anderson 2007).

Indeed, coastal and forested areas (as opposed to residential areas) have been the first to be grabbed by investors—whether or not they are under communal title. Presumably, this is because they don't (necessarily) involve "messy" evictions. Rather, communities are hemmed in little by little, increasingly losing access to vital common resources until livelihoods are so constrained that residential plots can be more easily bought off, one by one. This has been the case in the municipality of Trujillo, located on the Bay of Trujillo on the northern edge of Capiro Calentura National Park. In recent years, the area has been heavily targeted by investors, and was chosen as the site for a radical neoliberal experiment known as the "Charter City" (*ciudad modelo*) (See Box 6).

Since 2008, OFRANEH has denounced Canadian investor Randy Jorgenson—known as the "Porn King" for the industry in which he gained his fortune—and his company Life Vision Properties for illegally purchasing communal Garifuna lands around Trujillo. In collusion with the municipality, Jorgenson began by acquiring and enclosing a large stretch of Trujillo's coastline to begin construction on a cruise ship dock, the centerpiece of a mega-tourism complex (including hotels, boutiques and restaurants) called the "Banana Coast." The Garifuna community of Río Negro was the most immediately affected.[61] Cut off from the water, internally divided and under heavy harassment from project representatives, community members began selling their family plots to Life Vision Properties one by one

BOX 6. HONDURAS' CHARTER CITY: AN ASSAULT ON SOVEREIGNTY

In July 2011, the Honduran Congress approved legislation allowing for the creation of Special Development Regions (RED in Spanish), also known as "Charter Cities" (*ciudades modelos*) (La Prensa 2011). The first of these projects envisions a 33 km-squared city to be built within Honduran territory, but governed by foreign governments and investors (Spring 2011). The planned site of the new Charter City is the land in and around the northern coastal town of Trujillo, an area long coveted by investors as prime real estate for vacation homes and resort tourism. Preliminary studies for the project were funded by the IDB and Korean Agency for International Development (KOICA) (El Heraldo 2011c). Brainchild of US economist Paul Romer, the Charter City concept is an extreme take on the export processing zones created in the 1990s, except "larger in scale, broader in its scope for reform and far more innovative in its approach to governance" (Romer and Fuller 2011). Indeed, it has received high praises from maquila oligarchs such as Daniel Facussé, president of the Honduran Manufacturing Association (AHM) and member of the powerful Facussé clan (La Tribuna 2012a).

This Charter City is to be governed by an oddly named "Transparency Commission" composed of nine individuals appointed by president Lobo. The current interim commission consists of five economists and businesspeople (none of them Honduran) and chaired by Romer himself (ibid.). "Partner countries" in the developed world are to play a key role in providing "oversight, policing and jurisprudence" to "make the new city a more attractive place for would-be residents and investors" (Romer and Sánchez 2012). In a recent opinion piece in the *Globe and Mail*, Romer appealed to Canada to play this role, which would be compensated "using gains in the value of the land in the new reform zone" (ibid.). Partner countries would also lend security assistance, helping to make the City a "safe haven" from the insecurity that reigns outside its limits (Romer and Fuller 2011). According to the Economist (2011), prominent, libertarian-leaning entrepreneurs are linked with the project including Patri Friedman (grandson of Milton), Peter Thiel (founder of Paypal) and John Mackey (CEO of Whole Foods).

Who will live in this utopian city? According to Romer, forward-thinking, market-oriented Hondurans will vote with their feet, opting to move to the Charter City "out of enlightened self-interest" (ibid.). However, it is unclear whether this utopian project will come to fruition, or whether its regulatory framework will merely speed up a number of mega-development projects already in the pipeline, such as Canadian investor Randy Jorgenson's mega-tourism complex called "Banana Coast." For community-based movements like OFRANEH, the Charter City is a clear extension of the tourism mega-projects (as well as mega-energy and agribusiness projects) that have displaced, divided and criminalized Garifuna communities for over two decades. Claiming to target "undeveloped" and "uninhabited" land, this Charter City makes Garifuna residents—and their claims on land and ancestral territories—invisible. What's more, with the Canadian government potentially *governing* the enclave, and Canadian investors making windfall profits within it, the "Charter City" model looks remarkably like a new form of colonialism.

Garifuna leader Miriam Miranda commented, "it is difficult to get information, but it is evident that we're faced with the maximum expression of the loss of sovereignty" (Paley 2012). OFRANEH launched a National Campaign Against Charter Cities in July 2012.

until only six remained, watching their neighbors' houses being bulldozed to the ground (Spring 2011).[62]

Jorgenson and other investors also targeted the collectively managed forests around Trujillo, areas critical for watershed protection and sustainably harvesting food and other forest products. According to OFRANEH, many of the new projects will be built in the protected areas of the Capiro and Calentura mountains, causing deforestation and degradation in a zone that is highly vulnerable to natural disasters (Spring 2011; OFRANEH 2010b). Large areas, such as the future site of Jorgenson's "Campa Vista" vacation homes, have been enclosed with fences and private security, preventing community access. In the community of Guadalupe, lands acquired by Life Vision Properties at just over $50 per acre are being advertised in Canada starting at $30,000 per 0.4 acre plot (Spring 2011). What's more, the Trujillo area has been heavily militarized since the 2009 coup (a reality investors would rather keep under wraps). The Tumbador massacre (See Part Three), in which Miguel Facussé's private guards killed five peasants, occurred just 20 minutes away from one of Jorgenson's development sites (ibid.).

In projects like the "Banana Coast," Garífuna culture is either erased, substituted for Mayan culture (which is supposedly more appealing to foreign visitors) or repackaged as a tourist attraction. A brochure advertising the Los Micos Beach and Golf Resort[63] in Tela Bay reads:

> The barefoot elegance of this luxurious destination resort is your introduction to the beauty of this Undiscovered Coast. Discover a Central American paradise that blends the flavors, textures and traditions of Honduras' native Garífuna culture, yet provides the sophistication expected by international travelers.[64]

This combination of "discovery" and luxury invokes feel-good notions of corporate social and environmental responsibility. The brochure goes on to reassure tourists that "the visionaries of this luxurious "new frontier" remain ever-mindful of its cultural ancestry, abundant wildlife and natural wonderland." The "visionaries" behind Los Micos are the same business elites that now control the government. They include maquila owners Jacobo Kattán and Juan Canahuati; fast food and media mogul José Rafael Ferrari; and energy tycoon Freddy Násser (who is also Miguel Facussé's son-in-law) (Loperena 2010; Méndez 2009). The Los Micos resort—most of which is located inside Janet Kawas National Park[65]—is a public-private partnership, with basic infrastructure funded by the state (with a $35 million loan from the IDB for "sustainable tourism") and hotels and other tourist attractions funded by private investors (IDB 2005).

For Garifuna communities, aid-funded neoliberal initiatives such as land titling programs and conservation projects have not met their stated goals (tenure security and environmental sustainability). They have, however, succeeded in restructuring the northern coast to facilitate investment and accumulation by both international investors and the Honduran oligarchy. Indeed, Garifuna communities have been boxed in on all sides, with Facussé's oil palm and Dole's pineapple plantations; the enclosure of coastal waters and wilderness areas for tourism; the criminalization of subsistence activities; and the usurpation of community lands.

In the past, Garifuna organizations have rarely engaged in large-scale land occupations to reclaim their territories as seen in the Aguán. Rather, they have sought legal protection as tribal peoples through international human rights mechanisms. The IACHR, for instance, issued an injunction against Marbella on further developments in Triunfo de la Cruz. Garifuna radio stations—such as Faluma Bimetu (*Coco Dulce*) located in Triunfo— have played a critical role in informing communities of investment activities and organizing resistance while also preserving Garifuna language and music (Payne Roberts 2011). They have been especially important since the 2009 coup, which tightened censorship in the country and restricted information to the elite-controlled media.[66]

Due to increasing threats to their lands and livelihoods,

Garifuna organizations recently turned to the strategy of land occupation. On August 27, 2012 OFRANEH launched a 300-person occupation of a tract of ancestral Garifuna land called Vallecito, located within the planned Charter City and boxed in on the east, west and north by Facussé's heavily guarded oil palm plantations. The occupation hopes to gain international attention and pressure the government to recognize the legal titles of the Garifuna people and adhere to internationally binding conventions such as Convention 169 of the ILO.[67]

Carla García, legal advisor to the communities of Cristales and Río Negro, comments, "Everything points to the fact that Garifunas are not welcome in our own land; that we're not even welcome in this country; but this is where we were born and we're going to fight for our rights" (OFRANEH 2012).

PART 3

THE NEW AGUÁN MOVEMENTS: LAND, RESISTANCE AND FOOD SOVEREIGNTY

After the coup that overthrew Manuel Zelaya, our participation in the Resistance gave us even more awareness of the importance of recovering the land, not just in Aguán, but in the whole country. It strengthened our belief that on the land, we may not become rich, but at least we won't lack what we need to live; we'll have food, education and dignity.
—Unified Movement of Aguán Peasants (MUCA)
in "Machete de Esperanza" 2010

U nlike Nicaragua, Guatemala and El Salvador, Honduras did not see the emergence of a significant guerrilla movement (such as the Nicaraguan Sandinistas) in the 1970s and 80s. This is confounding, in a way, given its high levels of rural poverty and exploitation, especially at the hands of US fruit companies. The lack of a strong peasant insurgency in Honduras, however, can be explained in part by the combination of repressive and accommodating strategies used by the Honduran government to mediate social crisis (Mahoney 2001, 256). Thanks in part to the agrarian reforms of the 60s and 70s, levels of land concentration in Honduras were never as extreme as in neighboring countries where strong insurgencies emerged. As outlined in Part One, greater wage concessions and agrarian reform defused social demands to some degree, while the strong US-backed military repressed pockets of rebellion. This "stability" is also what made Honduras an attractive base for US counter-insurgency operations in the 1980s.

Nonetheless, it would be wrong to assume that Honduran peasants have not been active agents of social change. The victories they won in the 1960s and 70s, attest to the power of peasant movements. By the early 80s—due to the expansion of commercial agriculture and ranching, combined with population growth—the land question was rapidly worsening. In response, protests exploded throughout the country, demanding agrarian reform and stabilization of rising food prices (Envío 1997). The state responded in increasingly repressive ways. Reforms in the penal code increased fines and jail time for protest crimes such as peasant land invasions and street demonstrations (ibid.).

The National Coordinating Council of Peasant Unions (COCOCH) was formed in 1990 and remarkably survived the neoliberal assault on peasant unions, lands and livelihoods of the 1990s. In 1991, together with peasant leaders from six other countries, COCOCH founded the Association of Central American Peasant Organizations for Cooperation and Development (ASOCODE), an early precursor to the international peasant movement Vía Campesina, which now includes 149 member organizations in 69 countries (Boyer 2010; Edelman 2008). Vía Campesina—headquartered in Tegucigalpa from 1996-2004—is arguably the leading voice for peasants' rights and agrarian reform on the international stage, and is the intellectual author of the concept of "food sovereignty."[68]

In the Aguán, the abrupt reversal of agrarian reform in the early 1990s provoked a new wave of peasant organizing. But this was not the armed peasant insurgencies of the 1970s and 80s. Rather, the movements have engaged in a range of nonviolent tactics: from land occupations and negotiations to judicial appeals and legislative proposals. Only through terrific efforts at media manipulation (which are ongoing) could they be labeled "guerrillas." The Aguán movements made headway

under the administration of Manuel Zelaya: good faith negotiations between peasants and government agencies resulted in
Decree Law 18-2008 opening the possibility of granting legal
titles for communities that had farmed their lands for ten years
or more. The 2009 coup, however, abruptly closed off political
spaces opened up through decades of organizing, essentially forcing peasant movements to give up or scale up.

The shift from Zelaya's accommodating approach to the land
conflict to Lobo's militarized approach appears to have radicalized and unified the peasant movements. Their ongoing commitment to nonviolence, however, has subjected them to brutal, one-sided confrontations with police, military and private
guards. This assault on Aguán movements—and their courage
in the face of repression—has also inspired and informed the
National Front of Popular Resistance (FNRP), the broad-based
civil society coalition that emerged in opposition to the coup.
While far from ideological unity, the FNRP and its new political arm LIBRE (short for *Libertad y Refundación*, the Freedom
and Refoundation Party) have in turn provided a new national
platform for historic peasant demands.

Parts One and Two of this book provided a political economic
analysis of agrarian change in Honduras, especially during the
neoliberal and repressive turn of the last two decades. They
argued that these policies led to the growth of a powerful agro-
industrial oligarchy rooted in the three "boom" sectors of northern Honduras: maquilas, agribusiness and tourism. This class has
expanded its economic and political power through complex
mechanisms that squeezed peasant and indigenous livelihoods on
the one hand, and created new investment opportunities on the
other. The privatization of land and nature increasingly created
the conditions for "land grabs" and "green grabs" to occur with
impunity, under a veil of institutional legitimacy.

Part Three returns to the Aguán Valley and the social movements that have emerged from this new juncture in agrarian
politics. The new peasant movements, rooted in historic struggles for agrarian reform, go beyond traditional peasant demands.

Theirs is a radical critique of the dominant model and the institutionalized takeover of community-controlled food, land and markets by a globalized elite. Considering the strength of this movement, the stereotype, as Merryl (1995) puts it, of the "conservative nature of Honduran society, which is not conducive to a revolutionary uprising" seems all but obsolete. Speaking to these new conditions, LIBRE's motto says it all: *La Revolución es Inevitable en Honduras* (In Honduras, Revolution is Inevitable).

11
THE NEW CYCLE OF STRUGGLE: A SKETCH OF TWO AGUÁN MOVEMENTS

I decided to get organized and fight, because of how hard it is to feed our children. There are very few people who enjoy all of the country's wealth. So I joined the movement to fight for the land.
—Maribel García, Unified Movement of Aguán Peasants (MUCA)[69]

The extensive dispossession of peasants in the 1990s generated a new cycle in the history of peasant land struggles in the Aguán. Shattered cooperatives began mobilizing immediately to challenge the legality of the land grabs, submitting legal claims (*demandas de nulidad*) requesting the invalidation of the land sales. Some succeeded, but many others were stymied in the courts by the high-priced lawyers of Facussé and other elites. So, a number of cooperatives and landless families came together to form *movements*. With little political power vis-á-vis large landholders, a "new generation" of Aguán movements began strategically occupying lands they identified as designated for the collective use of the peasantry under the agrarian reform laws of 1961 and 1974. Since MCA was formed in 1999, dozens more followed, generating a patchwork of movements throughout the valley. MCA and MUCA, profiled below, are two of the pioneering and emblematic movements in this new cycle of struggle.

MCA—Peasant Movement of Aguán

One of the oldest in this "new generation" of Aguán movements, MCA's struggle is focused on reclaiming the lands of the
Regional Center for Military Training (known by its Spanish
acronym CREM), a former US-training camp for counter-
insurgency forces. The 5,724-hectare CREM has a long and
complex history of questionable land deals, and illustrates how
private capital repeatedly captures state resources and uses public
agencies as an instrument for profit, in violation of the social
aims of agrarian reform laws (See Box 7).

MCA carried out its first occupation at midnight on May 14,
1999 with 700 landless peasant families from around the country.
They called their new settlement on the former CREM site
"Guadalupe Carney" after a radical Jesuit priest from the U.S.
who helped organize Aguán cooperatives in the 1970s and was
later killed by counter-insurgency forces. The founding committee (*junta directiva*) of MCA was composed of three men
and two women from the four leading national peasant associations, including the Association of Peasant Women of Honduras
(AHMUC).[70] Compared to the first generation cooperatives
such as Salamá (see Chapter 13) almost entirely run by men,
the new Aguán movements have a much higher participation of
women in decision-making roles.[71]

Under pressure from MCA, as well as international humani-
tarian pressure following Hurricane Mitch, president Carlos
Flores Facussé (nephew of Miguel Facussé) awarded the first
1,500-hectare tract of former CREM lands to MCA in 2000.
Since then, additional portions of CREM lands have slowly been
adjudicated in favor of MCA based on successive congressional
decrees. Each wave of redistribution was accompanied by payment to the (illegal) landowner for his "improvements" (*mejo-
ras*) to the land (infrastructure, crops planted, etc.), a common
practice in Honduran land negotiations. All told, 105 million
lempiras (approximately US$5.25 million) in state funds were
authorized for paying off landowners and resolving the CREM
case (FIAN et al. 2011, 41). As Barnes and Riverstone (2008)

note, "the successful takeover of the CREM military base has been recognized as a 'transcendent event' indicating demand for the reactivation of an agrarian reform program in Honduras."

Of the original CREM lands, approximately 1,000 hectares (20 percent) remain to be titled to peasant families. These lands have been grabbed by Miguel Facussé, René Morales and congressman Oscar Nájera, and are the site of ongoing conflict. In March 2010, Facussé failed to appear in court on three separate occasions to account for his claim over 550 hectares known as the El Tumbador oil palm plantation (Ríos 2010b). To pressure the businessman, MCA peasants occupied El Tumbador on April 6, 2010, holding it for three months before being evicted. The occupation triggered a period of protracted negotiation between Facussé and INA for the payment of "improvements" (Ríos 2010). With no resolution in sight, however, MCA re-entered El Tumbador on November 15, 2010.

This time five peasants were fatally shot, and several injured, in a four-hour standoff with Facussé's security guards, employees of the Orion Security Company (El Heraldo 2010a).[73] Had Law 18-2008—which explicitly outlined the resolution of CREM—not been revoked, the bloodshed at El Tumbador might have been avoided.

Despite recent setbacks, MCA members are proud to have helped spawn and accompany a whole new generation of peasant movements, such as fellow Aguán movement MUCA (see below) and the peasant movement of Zácate Grande in southern Honduras, also battling Miguel Facussé.[74] Referring to this new cycle of struggle, Claudia Ruíz of the Coordinating Committee of Popular Organizations of Aguán (COPA) affirmed, "In 2000, the Aguán started a new phase in its history."[75]

MUCA—Unified Movement of Aguán Peasants

In 2001, shortly after the birth of MCA, the Unified Movement of Aguán Peasants (MUCA) was formed to demand the nullification of land sales and recover land for peasant families. At its inception, the movement was composed of three former peasant

BOX 7. HISTORY OF LAND DEALS AT FORMER CREM SITE[72]

1975: A US-Puerto Rican investor named Temístocles Ramírez de Arrellano purchases what would become the CREM site illegally for approximately **24 lempiras per hectare** (approximately US$4.86 per acre). Article 107 of the Honduran constitution prohibits foreigners from owning land within forty kilometers of the coast, where these lands are located.

1983: Ramírez is forced to give the land over to the US military for the creation of the CREM military training camp.

1990: After appealing to the US, Ramírez receives compensation from the Honduran government in the amount of 15,600,000 lempiras, a value of **2,275 lempiras per hectare** (approximately US$460.50 per acre), nearly 100 times the 1975 purchase price.

1993: CREM lands are reverted to the state for distribution to the peasantry by the National Agrarian Institute (INA) as mandated by the agrarian reform law, but the lands are never distributed. Instead, the municipality of Trujillo, where the land is located, sells the land to local cattle ranchers, politicians and military officials at the bargain price of **20 to 30 lempiras per hectare** (approximately US$1.25 – 1.87 per acre at the average exchange rate for that year).

1999: The Peasant Movement of Aguan (MCA) is formed, carrying out its first occupation and establishing the settlement of Guadalupe Carney on the former CREM site.

2000: The Public Prosecutor's office (*fiscalía*) brings charges against several municipal officials, including the mayor of Trujillo, for the illegal sale of state lands. President Flores Facussé awards the first 1,500-hectare tract of former CREM lands to MCA.

"Welcome brothers and sisters to territory liberated by MUCA" (photo by Greg McCain)

cooperatives looking to recuperate their lands. After a few years of organizing and researching various cases of illegal land acquisition, they had grown to 28 cooperatives (MUCA 2010a, 16). MUCA took its first legal action in 2004, filing seventeen requests for the nullification of land sales against Miguel Facussé, René Morales and Reinaldo Canales (ibid.). But under the conservative government of Ricardo Maduro (2002–2006)—famous for his "iron fist" (*mano dura*) policies—this approach mostly went nowhere.

In February 2006, 7,000 peasants blockaded the main road through Aguán, near the town of Tocoa, brandishing their machetes as a symbol of their identity as workers of the land. The protest, known as the "occupation of the five thousand machetes" (*la toma de los cinco mil machetes*) succeeded in getting a government representative to visit the region and commit to carrying out an investigation of the fraudulent land deals. The occupation marked a turning point for MUCA and the launch of a new strategy of public protest and strategic negotiation

(MUCA 2010a; FIDH 2011). In its boldest action to date, the movement occupied a Facussé-owned palm oil processing plant in early June 2009. After holding it for six days, president Manuel Zelaya made a personal visit to the Aguán to negotiate MUCA's evacuation and sign an agreement towards the resolution of the land disputes (ibid.).

This momentous victory led to the creation of a special commission—composed of representatives from the executive office, MUCA, INA, the Secretary of Agriculture (SAG) and large landowners—to resolve the MUCA case. But signs of the impending coup loomed large. On June 23, unidentified gunmen in Tocoa shot MUCA advisor and commission member Fabio Evelio Ochoa four times in an assassination attempt. Ochoa had also been an outspoken supporter of the popular referendum slated for June 28, and had been working on a case to win compensation for 900 former farmworkers poisoned by agrochemicals used by the Standard Fruit Company (Defensores en Línea 2009). The coup d'état on June 28, 2009 decimated the commission and any progress made under Zelaya towards resolving the MUCA case.

Clearly intending to end the process of popular consultation, including negotiations with peasant movements, the coup inadvertently sowed the seeds of popular resistance. The coup's "awakening" of civil society, as it is often put by Hondurans, created an unprecedented articulation of formerly atomized, even conflicting, social movements. Students, teachers, industrial workers' unions, human rights organizations, indigenous peoples, peasants, feminists, LGBT communities, artists and faith-based groups were galvanized by the coup and the repression that followed, coming together to form the FNRP (see Box 8).

The coup did not succeed in destroying the peasant movements. With the backing of the popular resistance movement, MUCA felt empowered to take even bolder action:

> We called a meeting [after the coup] and started talking about taking stronger measures... We felt stronger, and

> when you're stronger, you can carry a bigger load on
> your back. We had the power now because we were
> many and also because we had the support of the
> National Front of Popular Resistance. (MUCA 2010a)

In early December of 2009, MUCA's 2,500 member families launched a massive occupation of 21 oil palm plantations in
protest of the broken pre-coup agreement. The Lobo government—elected in November 2009 in elections widely boycot-
ted by grassroots movements and international election observers—responded by sending more than 2,000 troops into the
region, the first of several waves of militarization. Negotiations
took place under these tense conditions, leading to a new agreement signed on April 14, 2010 promising to grant MUCA a
total of 11,000 hectares and government resources for education, health and housing construction (MUCA 2010a, 40). Six
MUCA members were murdered during the course of these
negotiations, demonstrating the extreme pressure applied on
peasant movements to sign agreements that are detrimental to
their interests (FIDH 2011).

Ousted president Manuel Zelaya (seated) visits a MUCA settlement after his
return from exile in 2011 (photo by Jesse Freeston)

BOX 8. THE FNRP: ROOTS AND EVOLUTION OF A SOCIAL MOVEMENT

by Tyler Shipley[76]

In response to neoliberal policies, a number of regional activist networks emerged in the mid-1990s to address local problems—e.g. the Civic Council of Popular and Indigenous Organizations of Honduras (COPINH) in Intibucá, the Environmental Movement of Olancho (MAO) and labor activists in the capital (*Bloque Popular*). These organizations soon recognized, however, that a broad challenge to corruption and structural inequality required a *national* movement. In the early 2000s, regional groups began organizing coordinated events, which culminated in a 10-hour blockade of all four major highways into Tegucigalpa in 2003.

Out of that successful action, the *Coordinadora Nacional de Resistencia Popular* (National Coordinating Committee of Popular Resistance or CNRP) was formed, which rotated its leadership between different member groups. With a national network and growing popular support, the CNRP became an increasingly significant force in Honduran politics, and the movement achieved its greatest gains under president Zelaya, including an increase in the minimum wage, a moratorium on new mining concessions, protection of women's access to contraceptives, recognition of peasant claims to land and steps towards refounding the Honduran constitution.

Shortly after the June 2009 coup, the CNRP was converted into the *Frente Nacional de Resistencia Popular* (National Front of Popular Resistance or FNRP) in order to include the many Hondurans who were "awakened" and radicalized by the coup and took to the streets in peaceful, but determined, defiance of the military regime. The immediate task of the

FNRP was to have the president reinstated, but—rooted in the social movements struggling against neoliberalism for years—it never lost sight of the broader goal, which was the refoundation of Honduras from the ground up, beginning with the constitutional assembly.

The FNRP was the central organ of social movements after the coup. It organized a nationwide boycott of the November 2009 post-coup elections and maintained a strong and unified front against the Porfirio Lobo regime for the first two years. But under the combined pressures of unrelenting repression, activist burnout and lack of resources and international support, the FNRP showed signs of splintering in 2011 and 2012, especially around the strategic question of whether to participate in the 2013 elections or to boycott them and keep the movement in the streets.

Participation in the electoral process was championed by former president Zelaya, who returned to Honduras in May 2011.[77] While Zelaya's return injected energy and hope into the movement, it also gave him tremendous influence over a movement of which he was never originally a part. Under Zelaya's leadership, the FNRP resolved to create a new political party, LIBRE, to participate in elections. Many in the movement were disheartened by the decision, and created the *Espacio Refundacional* (Refoundational Space), a sub-group committed to keeping power mobilized in communities rather than channeled into the realm of electoral politics, which could be co-opted by traditional politicians.

Nevertheless, most activists in the FNRP recognized that the only way to keep LIBRE accountable to social movements would be to participate in it. With broad popular participation, LIBRE came to encompass diverse currents, some close to the FNRP and others closer to the traditional Liberal party. While it remains unclear which currents will ultimately dominate the party, the "refoundation" of Honduras along democratic and participatory lines remains central to the FNRP's project, and its participation in the electoral process is one of many strategies to achieve that aim.

As part of the agreement, MUCA scaled down its occupation to six plantations on approximately 3,000 hectares (MUCA 2010a; Ríos 2010). Life in the new settlements was extremely hard, with no shelter, sewage, potable water or access to food. The peasants survived by selling palm fruit and by organizing in solidarity with nearby communities to get water. But the plantations were in poor condition, and the yields subpar. The oil palm trees had been neglected by the large growers who had likely seen the writing on the wall, investing little in disputed lands they risked losing (MUCA 2010a, 46). Peasant mobility was (and continues to be) restricted by the heavy police, military and private security presence, making travel on the long, dusty plantation roads a dangerous endeavor.

While there are few illusions that the Lobo government will negotiate in good faith and honor its agreements with peasants, the April 2010 MUCA agreement is seen as a breakthrough. MUCA's fearlessness has also inspired numerous other movements in the region and beyond. Members of the Isletas cooperative, for instance, who lost their lands to Standard Fruit in 1990, re-occupied the land in January 2012. One Isletas member commented, "If the peasants of MUCA can do it in the Aguán Valley on the oil palm plantations of Miguel Facussé, then the peasants of Isletas can do it too" (OlanchitoNoticias 2012).

12
RESISTING FRAGMENTATION, CONSTRUCTING UNITY

The state-sponsored colonization of the Aguán in the 1960s and 70s, as noted in Part One, was not a "genuine" agrarian reform. It was, as many resettlement programs around the world—such as those carried out by military governments in Indonesia and Brazil in the same period—a way of containing or diffusing peasant demands while avoiding a real transformation of agrarian power. On the one hand, the stronger, more organized groups are treated as the proverbial "squeaky wheel" that gets the grease (e.g. land concessions, access to credit, government assistance, etc.) in exchange for demobilizing their bases. On the other hand, unorganized communities and smaller movements—which are less connected to regional, national and international networks—can be more easily repressed with little attempt at appeasement by the state.

Thus, with "agrarian reform" and cooperativization used as tools for rural control, the Aguán movements have been highly vulnerable to fragmentation. When MUCA signed its agreement with the Lobo government in April 2010, for instance, a group of peasants belonging to four former cooperatives refused to sign, splintering off and forming the Authentic Movement for the Re-vindication of Aguán Peasants (MARCA). Unlike the others, which had sold their titles to investors in the early 1990s, MARCA's cooperatives still held the original land titles received through the agrarian reform (hence the name "authentic"). They felt that signing the agreement risked weakening their position in ongoing court cases (Bird 2012). Another agreement signed by MUCA in June 2011 was rejected by peasants of the "left bank" (*margen izquierda*) of the Aguán River, leading to a split between MUCA-MI (Left Bank) and MUCA-MD (Right Bank) (ibid.).

These divisions left MARCA and MUCA-MI extremely vulnerable to repression. After their refusal to accept the terms of the June 2011 agreement, the fourteen cooperatives that make up MUCA-MI began receiving anonymous threats. The following month, death squads assassinated three MUCA-MI peasant leaders.[78] The killings were accompanied by a rash of defamatory statements in the elite-controlled press, accusing MUCA-MI of criminal activity and blaming them for the escalating violence in Aguán (Paz 2011). This served to brand MUCA-MD (which had signed the government's proposed agreement) as compliant "good peasants" and MUCA-MI (which refused to sign) as deviant "bad peasants."

Despite ongoing negotiations, which in some cases yield positive results, large landowners rarely comply with agreements, and the agro-elite-supported government rarely enforces them. Rather, comments Claudia Ruíz (COPA), "negotiations are often used as a way to identify movement leaders to target for repression."[79] Additionally, most agreements are unfavorable, if not outright detrimental, to peasants' interests. The agreements are generally based on the landowners' willingness to sell, and at an inflated value determined mostly by their own appraisers. In recent rounds of negotiation with MUCA and MARCA, the agrarian reform agency (INA) has functioned as an intermediary with private banks, to broker a loan to the peasant movements to purchase the lands from Facussé. MUCA General Secretary Yoni Rivas remarks:

> It is a scheme to undermine our struggle and eliminate us. They failed in their attempt to exterminate us with guns, so now they're taking another shot [at] us, trying to strangle us *financially* to drive us off our lands. (Trucchi 2012, emphasis added)

The loan agreements ensure that peasants (and their lands) will remain shackled to oil palm production if they ever hope to repay their debts. Moreover, they often stipulate that agricultural inputs must be obtained from the large landowner, and palm fruit must be sold to his processing plants. These "co-investment" (*co-inversión*) or joint venture provisions are a holdover from the 1992 Agricultural Modernization Law. They guarantee that Facussé, Morales and other palm oil tycoons will retain a steady supply of raw materials.[80] Ríos (2010) compares these deals to the outgrower schemes of United Fruit, which began contracting independent producers and cooperatives in the 1950s. In this way, the company locked in production while avoiding all of the risks and burdens associated with owning a large plantation (labor strikes, natural disasters, etc.).

Considering these negotiating conditions, and the brazen human rights violations that continue virtually unabated, Aguán movements have recognized two important things: 1) the need to become more united in the face of repression and divisive state strategies, and 2) the need to participate in the national resistance (FNRP), both to lend peasant support to the national movement and to make sure agrarian reform remains a priority within it. These two points are significant considering the historic fragmentation of the peasant movement, rife with internal division fueled by US intervention and military repression.

The National Federation of Honduran Peasants (FENACH), founded in the mid-1950s, was one of the first peasant associations in Honduras. In the wake of agrarian reform in the early 1960s, the US State Department, working with the AFL-CIO, established the parallel National Association of Honduran Peasants (ANACH) in an attempt to counter the influence of FENACH and push the peasant movement in a pro-US, anti-Communist direction (Frank 2010). After the military overthrow of president Villeda Morales in 1963, FENACH was heavily repressed by security forces, its offices destroyed and its leaders imprisoned (Barry 1991).

In opposition to the conservative influence of ANACH,

peasant cooperatives, landless workers and independent producers in the Lower Aguán Valley formed the National Union
of Peasant Workers (CNTC) in 1985. CNTC, and indeed all
peasant organizations, were severely weakened in the 1990s by
neoliberalism and Hurricane Mitch. Nonetheless, ANACH and
CNTC remain two of the strongest peasant unions in Aguán.
Both MUCA and MCA are affiliated with the more progressive
CNTC, which is in turn associated with the COCOCH at the
national level and Vía Campesina at the international level.

As Boyer (2010) points out, however, the relationship between
the grassroots movements in the remote Aguán region and the
national and transnational organizations of which they are a part
has often been tense:

> Unfortunately, as the gaze of the Honduran peasant
> movement shifted globally to play a vital part of creating
> Vía Campesina, many of the unions' ties with their bases
> languished. The charges of excessive careerism play
> into this; many see in the national leadership a pursuit
> of personal advancement, material gain, and personal
> power over and above servicing the broader social goals
> of their unions. (335)

Of course, the difficulty of bridging grassroots reality and global
advocacy is a challenge for all social movements, particularly in
the face of repression and divisive negotiating strategies such as
those outlined above.[81] In post-coup Honduras, however, the
Lobo government's ruthless repression has paradoxically served
as an unassailable point of unity—in the Aguán and beyond. For
instance, a Congress Against Militarization (*Encuentro contra la
Militarización*) was held in Tocoa in October 2011. Attended by
over 450 people from around the country, the event aimed to
raise national awareness about the militarization of the region
and build solidarity with the Aguán. The event took place in the
midst of a "third wave" of militarization of the Aguán since the
coup, a deployment known as Operation Xatruch II.

Peasant Congress in Tocoa with representatives from various Aguán movements, January 2012 (photo by Aryeh Shell)

During the congress, the idea emerged of forming a permanent human rights observatory to provide on-the-ground support for communities facing repression and eviction from their lands. It would also serve to unify the movements and various human rights and grassroots development initiatives, creating a central clearinghouse for collecting testimonies; sending out communiqués to the press and alerts to national and international allies; and providing training to communities to use the internet and community radio stations to break the media silence.[82] With a sense of urgency created by Xatruch II, the idea was quickly turned into action. The International Human Rights Observatory of Aguán was inaugurated on November 11, 2011, housed temporarily in a one-room community center in a residential neighborhood of Tocoa. The Observatory is co-sponsored by all of the Aguán movements—plus representatives from the FNRP, the indigenous group COPINH, the Garifuna organization OFRANEH and other national and international organizations (See Appendix: Declaration of the International Human Rights Observatory of Aguán).

Subsequent meetings held in Tocoa have functioned to bring together diverse, even conflicting, Aguán movements and their allies under one roof to address pressing human rights concerns. The Observatory—and other spaces and gatherings focused on human rights—have simultaneously created grassroots spaces for collective analysis: of the state's divisive strategies, of the movements' shared interests, and of the broader vision for agrarian reform and food sovereignty. Vía Campesina, while still viewed somewhat ambivalently by Aguán peasants, has stepped in to mobilize international support against repression in the region. While tensions remain, the militarized repression of Aguán has paradoxically created the conditions for diverse peasant groups to converge and work on crafting a much bolder vision within the framework of national resistance and international solidarity.

13
PEASANT-CONTROLLED PALM OIL: THE CASE OF SALAMÁ

Here in the Aguán almost everyone is indebted to his neighborhood
food store (pulpería), because the salary we earn is miserable. The
large landowners said oil palm would bring progress, development
and benefits for the people, but the only progress that occurred was for
them and not for workers.
—Isaías, oil palm plantation worker[83]

With 1.7 to 2 million people worldwide working in the palm oil sector in 2006, supporters praise the industry for generating rural employment through a combination of jobs on large plantations and in downstream processing, as well as through outgrower schemes that incorporate smallholders into corporate value chains (World Growth 2011, 13). Indeed, oil palm provides more employment than other agro-export crops such as soybeans. In Brazil, for instance, one worker can farm 250 hectares of soybeans, while a mechanized palm oil plantation in Malaysia requires one worker for every 12 hectares (Clay 2004, 182).[84] Questions of quality of life, economic dependence and control over value chains, however, are rarely discussed. The peasant-controlled oil palm sector in the Aguán offers a useful perspective from which to assess the industry's "job creation" claims.

Worker testimonies from the Aguán reveal extremely pre-carious working conditions and poor quality of communal life in areas controlled by large plantation owners (See Box 9). One plantation worker states that, since the re-concentration of Aguán lands, "the money supply throughout the Aguán has decreased dramatically" as private companies extract wealth from local communities (Trucchi 2010). The *peasant-owned* oil palm cooperatives, however, created in the 1970s through the agrarian reform project, offer a starkly different picture. Few of these cooperatives remain after the neoliberal land grabs of the 1990s, but those that do, such as the Salamá cooperative, provide inspiration and material support for the broader peasant movement.

Visiting the community of Suyapa, in the heart of the Aguán, is like entering another world. Compared to the living conditions common in the rest of the region, it almost looks like a middle-class suburb, with brightly painted homes, satellite dishes, fruit trees, gardens and pickup trucks in semi-detached garages. Suyapa residents are all members, or family of members, of the Salamá cooperative, one of only fourteen original, peasant-owned palm oil cooperatives in the Aguán that survived neoliberalism.

Suyapa settlers began arriving in the 1960s as poor migrants from the north and west of the country, naming their community after the Virgin of Suyapa, patron saint of Honduras. Like most Aguán settlers who came from traditional farming backgrounds, they began growing food staples or *granos básicos,* primarily corn, until they were induced by the government to cultivate oil palm (Macías 2001, 80). Suyapa is said to be the first peasant settlement to receive training in oil palm production from the National Agrarian Institute (INA). According to Macías (2001), INA extensionists arrived from Tegucigalpa in April 1970, and in May of that year the Salamá cooperative was born, giving the community access to credit, training and markets for oil palm through the government (IDB-funded) program.

Salamá currently consists of 66 member families, who collectively manage 1,800 hectares (4,400 acres) primarily of oil palm, with some livestock and small parcels of corn and beans.[86] In addition to its members, Salamá also employs 200-300 workers

BOX 9. PLANTATION WORKERS SPEAK OUT

From a report by Giorgio Trucchi (correspondent for Rel-UITA and ALBA SUD)[85]

"I was working 8 hours a day harvesting palm fruit and had to meet the quotas imposed by the plantation managers. If I failed to deliver the fruit on time, I had to stay until I was done. It is very hard work. It was very hot and we were given only fifteen minutes to eat and drink. When I ran out of water, all I could do was drink standing-water from puddles. We could not stop because the foremen reported any delay to the managers, who would then reprimand or fire us... We were sold the idea that this monoculture was going to guarantee jobs and wellbeing for everyone, but all it brought us was unemployment and poverty." —Daniel, former worker for Miguel Facussé

"They would hire you for a trial period of two months and then you were fired. Then they would tell you to come back within 45 days and you'd get hired again. In this way, we had no rights to anything. We had no benefits, no insurance, no health coverage. If we ever tried to form unions or demand wage increases, we were fired. For cutting down the fruit bunches, I was paid 75 lempiras (less than $4 USD) for one ton of palm fruit. To do weeding and cleaning the underbrush, the payment was 1 lempira per block (16 square meters) and 100 lempiras for applying toxic chemicals." —Santos, plantation worker

"I worked in farm maintenance, applying pesticides. We used all kinds of chemicals such as Roundup, Gramoxone and Paraquat, and when we finished applying them, the foreman would tell us to wash the tank out in a nearby stream. At first, they gave us something to protect ourselves, but then they said it was too expensive and let us work without any protection. They never gave us boots, rubber gloves or even aprons; only tiny masks so tight they made you suffocate. One day, the valve broke on a tank I was carrying and I was completely drenched [in chemicals]. I told the foreman and the manager that I felt sick, but they just ignored me and said go back to work. That night I got extremely ill and had to be hospitalized. If it weren't for some nuns who helped cover the medical costs, I wouldn't be here now telling you this story." —Isaías, plantation worker

annually. This equates to approximately one worker per six to nine hectares of cropped oil palm, a higher rate of employment than the above-cited employment rate on a Malaysian plantation (one worker per 12 hectares). Aside from the number of jobs the cooperative provides, there is evidence that these jobs provide better working conditions and are more supportive of peasant farming capabilities. In a study of corporate oil palm expansion in northern Guatemala, Alonso-Fradejas (2012) found that peasant workers would rather work for other peasants than for agribusiness, for a number of reasons: lunch was normally provided, foremen did not harass them and the workday was generally shorter. The latter was especially important, since it allowed them to earn a wage and still have time to farm their own small plots and tend to community and family needs (15). With rising food prices, this ability to supplement one's wage with self-grown food can be critical.

Salamá also manages a plant for producing crude palm oil, which it sells to another peasant-owned plant (Hondupalma) that has the refining capacity to manufacture edible oil. Thanks to a donation by the Colombian government under Zelaya in 2009, Salamá now also has the capacity to produce biodiesel for on-site use.[87] Through the collectively managed funds generated by the sale of palm oil, Suyapa residents receive housing, water, sewage, electricity and even cable TV. With some government support, the community also provides free education through the ninth grade, and primary health care is available for all members and workers at a community health post.

As with most cooperatives in the region, the late 1990s and early 2000s were difficult for Salamá. Pressure for members to sell land to investors was high, a temptation first sparked by the AML of 1992 and magnified by Hurricane Mitch in 1998. The hurricane destroyed houses, infrastructure and oil palms. Between 1998 and 2000, Salamá's production dropped by 53 percent and by 2001 the cooperative faced a debt of 69 million lempiras (US$4.6 million) (Macías 2001).

When asked how Salamá made it through this period, cooperative members point to their organizational efforts and collective ethic. Anyone openly contemplating selling his land, or encouraging others to do so, was immediately expelled from the organization. The co-op board is elected by general assembly and receives pay and benefits equal to all other members and workers. After the hurricane, those associates who remained invested a tremendous amount of labor in re-planting oil palms, re-building

A home in the community of Suyapa, where residents are members of the Salamá peasant palm oil cooperative (photo by T. Kerssen)

the cooperative to be stronger than before. Notably, Suyapa bans the sale and consumption of alcohol in the community, which is thought to encourage wasteful spending, conflicts and divisions.

Salamá offers an example of a socially oriented palm enterprise, rooted in democratic ownership and participation. It stands in stark contrast to the expansionist private palm oil corporations that offer no benefit to communities except few, poorly paid jobs. There are other examples of the social benefits of peasant-controlled palm oil in the Aguán, as well. In addition to providing all of the same benefits as Salamá, the peasant cooperative Prieta provides full college scholarships to all the children of member families. None of the children of Prieta associates have migrated to the United States—an extreme rarity for rural Honduras.[88] Peasant-owned Hondupalma provides free transportation to all associates and workers (a huge advantage to peasants living in remote areas); runs its own full service hospital with the help of Cuban medical staff; and provides free rations of its products to associates, workers and independent producers.[89]

Additionally, peasant-owned cooperatives in the Aguán see their social mission as extending to the broader movement. For instance, by choosing to buy palm fruit from the peasant movement MUCA, Salamá provides a critical marketing channel outside the dominant private processors (e.g. Dinant, Jaremar). While not directly engaged in the land conflicts, their solidarity with peasant movements makes them targets of repression and marginalization. The palm oil brand Exquisita, produced by Coapalma—an association of 13 peasant cooperatives (all of the surviving Aguan co-ops minus Salamá, which stands alone)—is barred from elite-controlled supermarket chains, allegedly due to its link to peasant movements.[90] In addition, a number of leaders from these first generation cooperatives have been assassinated during the post-coup militarization, including Prieta's president and treasurer, both killed in February 2011, and Coapalma's president, killed in July 2011.[91]

The intense violence suffered by co-op leaders since the coup, side by side with the peasant movements, attests to the co-ops' strategic importance and substantive difference from corporate plantations. Salamá and the other original cooperatives formed in the 1970s and 80s are living remnants (and reminders) of an earlier wave of agrarian reform. As such, they provide an alternative model, material support and key alliances for younger organizations and movements in the region. To be sure, their production model remains rooted in the chemical-intensive methods advanced in the 1960s–80s; the ecological and health impacts of this model remain a serious concern. In contrast with corporate plantations, however, which are the source of widespread repression and displacement in the region, the cooperative palm sector is aligned with peasant movements in promoting a community-controlled economy throughout the Aguán. And this movement, more and more, is evolving towards a vision that embraces agro-ecology and food sovereignty.

14
FROM PALM OIL TO FOOD SOVEREIGNTY

At one time a diverse ecosystem sustaining small peasant and indigenous communities, northern Honduras was transformed in the 20th century into an agro-industrial landscape. As Boyer and Pell (1999) note, "peasants from the north coast became banana workers, losing their cultural ties to small-scale peasant agriculture and to nature itself" (39). The same can be said of the Aguán oil palm cooperatives created in the 1970s, which tied peasants—not only from the north, but migrants from all over the country—to the input-intensive production of an exportable cash crop. While Aguán peasants have always grown subsistence crops inasmuch as they were able, their fate primarily lied with oil palm. Consequently, Aguán struggles have largely focused on the right to control and benefit from oil palm, the region's most economically important crop.

In contrast, neoliberal discourse (e.g. of the World Bank, USAID, IDB) focuses on "economic growth" and "employment" in the sector, but rarely on who controls the value chain. The few Aguán cooperatives that survived the restructuring policies of 1990s show that, in fact, *peasant-controlled* operations can be highly beneficial to community wellbeing. By comparison, outgrower schemes or agreements that otherwise bind small-holders to large processing companies deepen peasant debt and dependence.

In the Aguán, this debate goes back to the very origins of

agrarian reform. The radical North American priest James Guadalupe Carney, who worked closely with Aguán peasants in the 1970s, was an outspoken critic of the government's aid-funded cooperativization program, arguing it created dependence, not autonomy, in the countryside. In his autobiography *To be a Revolutionary*, published posthumously in 1985, Carney observed:

> Who are the real beneficiaries of agrarian reform in Honduras? It is the gringos. They have the biggest business in the world lending us the money for agrarian reform. With this money we buy machinery, petroleum, and many other things from them. When the co-ops finally produce the fruit of the palm tree, who will have the biggest part of the profit from its final product? The gringos of the US Standard Fruit Company.[92] (Jeffrey 2002, 40)

Some peasant cooperatives did win control over processing plants and marketing boards through hard-fought struggles. Others, such as the Isletas cooperative, were heavily repressed for taking steps towards greater autonomy. After trying to bypass Standard Fruit to market directly to consumers, the Fourth Infantry Battalion headed by Colonel Gustavo Álvarez entered Isletas in February 1977, accusing the co-op of communism and throwing its leaders in jail (New Internationalist 1982). A new, favorable contract with Standard Fruit was quickly signed. Álvarez was later revealed to have been on the company's payroll.

Few Aguán cooperatives survived the structural adjustment policies of the early 1990s. The peasant-controlled oil palm operations that did remain—such as Prieta and Salamá—are a model to which Aguán movements aspire. Nonetheless, many have also begun to question the wisdom of industrial monoculture. Eduardo Flores, Aguán peasant and leader in the CNTC commented:

Honduras has lost its food sovereignty because the state tells us what to plant and what not to plant. They've incentivized peasants through state-funded training to plant all of their land to oil palm, because they say it's the wave of the future. But what will we eat tomorrow? What will happen when there is over-production, and it can't be sold because the market is saturated? And what about the land? If you take a plantation and you pull out the oil palms, you need twenty years for the soil to regenerate before you can plant corn, beans and other food crops again.[93]

Likewise, MUCA (2010) reflects:

We have to consider whether the exclusive cultivation of African oil palm is the best choice. It generates income, but it doesn't produce food for us or for our communities. African palm was imposed on us in the 1970s and we shouldn't forget that it was the central axis of a false agrarian reform passed by military governments... Moreover, the agrochemicals that are used to maintain its production contaminate the Aguán River and the lands that we could use to plant other crops. (49-50)

The national resistance movement has also taken up the banner of food sovereignty, albeit gradually, connecting the dots between repression in the countryside and junk food in the supermarkets (Trucchi and Zelaya 2010). Following the massacre of MCA peasants at El Tumbador in 2010, the FNRP launched a nation-wide consumer boycott of Facussé-owned food brands (e.g. Dixie, Yummies and Zibas snacks; Mazola cooking oil; Íssima condiments and prepared soups, etc.). The boycott has been disseminated online, through blogs and social media, and via neighborhood outreach. The group Artists in Resistance (*Artistas en Resistencia*), part of the FNRP, lent its efforts to the campaign, creating provocative public art, graffiti and music to circumvent the elite-controlled media and get the word out. One poster shows an oozing ketchup packet with the brand name *Íssima;* a closer look reveals the ketchup is meant to be blood, with a label that reads, "100 percent spilled blood of innocent peasants" (AenR 2010). A rap song about the boycott was produced by Artists in Resistance and shared online, with the lyrics playing on the word "íssima":

> Facussé, I won't consume any more of your trash; They say you're the one, who's invading all these lands, that don't belong to you; but it's over now; We're going to hit you hard with the resistance. Your food is *malÍSSIMA* (terrible); your conscience *apestosÍSSIMA* (stinks). The counter-culture is struggling for a better Honduras![94]

Concerns about the corporate control of food were sharpened by the 2008 global food crisis and subsequent coup, which caused an upsurge in food prices. The FAO (2011) indicates that the price of corn in the country has increased sharply, exceeding the highest levels seen in 2008, and the price of beans has remained at crisis levels. In a country with an estimated 375,000 landless peasant families and a 77 percent rural poverty rate, high food prices rapidly compound rural hunger (Vía Campesina et al. 2011).

In this context, MUCA has begun focusing increasingly on the production of "basic grains" (*granos básicos*), referring primarily to corn and beans, the staples of the Honduran diet. On the lands it has been able to recover in the past few years, MUCA established a number of "food sovereignty projects" focused on food production and distribution. So far, they have planted mostly corn and beans (annual crops), but are gradually planting yuca, plantain and pineapple (perennial crops), indicating a longer-term investment in the land.[95] The projects are intended to eventually provide employment to young people in the region to prevent the out-migration of youth, as well as reduce dependence on expensive imported food, or foods produced by the agro-oligarchs they are fighting against.[96] MUCA member Consuelo comments:

> About 50 percent of what we eat is nutritious food, food we grew ourselves, like corn, beans, some vegetables. Right now there are many health epidemics in the occupied territories. Too many! Our families aren't accustomed to living where they are so vulnerable, where so many chemicals have been dumped in the ground. We are trying not to eat certain foods that both help our enemy and are very harmful to our health. (Elliot 2012)

MUCA has provided production support to younger movements such as the Peasant Movement of Orica, a settlement of 300 families on lands occupied in September 2010, which is now producing *granos básicos* for self-sufficiency. The movement is also working to establish a network of small food markets (*consumos*) to distribute local produce at low cost.[97] In recognition of their struggle for land and food sovereignty, which has inspired movements in Honduras and throughout the Americas, in October 2012, the US Food Sovereignty Alliance awarded MUCA the fourth annual Food Sovereignty Prize in 2012.[98]

Nevertheless, none of the Aguán movements, including MUCA, have abandoned oil palm completely as a development tool. In fact, the sale of palm fruit to the Salamá processing plant since 2010 has financed many of MUCA's projects, from *granos básicos*, livestock and pisciculture (fisheries) to bakeries and woodworking, welding and autobody shops (CESPAD et al. 2011, 26). These are not just agricultural or food projects; they are *economic diversification* projects aiming at putting whole economies back in the hands of local communities and families. Oil palm remains a strategic part of this vision—specifically, oil palm that is peasant-controlled from production to processing to retail. One young peasant leader even jokingly proposed replacing John Deere

Makeshift home on a MUCA-occupied oil palm plantation with corn and squash production (photo by T. Kerssen)

with MUCA-brand tractors someday, manufactured by and for Aguán peasants.[99]

Aguán movements may not have rejected oil palm production or fully embraced agroecology, but they *are* engaged in an ongoing discussion about food sovereignty among themselves and with transnational movements like Vía Campesina. But in the Aguán (and indeed everywhere), food sovereignty has to be pragmatic. It has to work *now*, if imperfectly, in the embattled context in which peasants find themselves. Before devoting all of their resources to producing food, shattered local markets—destroyed by neoliberal policies—have to be slowly rebuilt. To this end, MUCA is working to establish a network of local stores to distribute affordable, locally grown food in the Aguán... but it's an uphill battle. In January 2012, for instance, without state purchasing or functioning distribution mechanisms, 696 quintales (69,600 lbs) of corn sat idle in Orica. "We don't have a market," said peasant leader Adelio Muñoz, "without a market, we can't keep farming basic grains."[100]

Therefore, oil palm—an economically important crop with

secure markets, infrastructure, access to credit and distribution channels—remains strategic to the peasant movements of the Aguán. It is a pragmatic component of their long-term struggle for land and food sovereignty.

This long-term vision is also reflected in a new policy proposal put forward by a coalition of peasant movements, including MUCA, MCA, COPA, Vía Campesina, COPINH, OFRANEH and a number of other farmers' associations and non-governmental organizations (NGOs). On October 11, 2011, the coalition submitted the proposed law, called the Integrated Agrarian Transformation Law (*Ley de Transformación Agraria Integral*), to the National Congress. Intended to replace and abolish the 1992 AML, the law is ambitious. In addition to the redistribution of land, it outlines the state's responsibility *inter alia* to:

- Prioritize domestic food production by small, medium and cooperative producers for domestic consumption
- Prohibit the production, experimental trials or sale of genetically modified seed and support the conservation of native and creole seeds by peasants and indigenous groups
- Create public institutions dedicated to providing credit and technical assistance to peasant producers
- Establish culturally appropriate rural education centers for training young people in forestry, agriculture and peasant culture and economy
- Eliminate the exploitation of agricultural workers and prohibit the contamination of the air, waterways and other natural resources (Vía Campesina et al. 2011)

Perhaps most importantly, Article 2 of the proposed law stipulates that agrarian reform must be part of a comprehensive policy framework that is in harmony with other national policies concerning education, health, housing, employment, infrastructure, trade and finance.

Past agrarian reform policies have been far from "integrated." Rather, they have been used as means of rural control and containment of peasant movements. In a study of state-led agrarian reform in Brazil, for example, Wright (2003) explains how the "government's strategy was to allow just enough agrarian reform in major trouble spots to keep the movement from spreading or taking on regional or national significance... Agrarian reform programs were just a pressure relief valve to forestall genuine or generalized reform" (275). What's more, peasant-oriented agrarian policies are often a drop in the bucket compared to policies and subsidies favoring industrialization. In many countries, this contradiction has generated what Kay (2008) calls an "agriculture of two velocities": On the one hand, a struggling peasant sector with little access to credit, local markets or social services; and on the other, a thriving, export-oriented agro-industrial sector absorbing the majority of state resources. Under these conditions, peasants struggle to eke out an existence and become an easily exploitable pool of laborers for agribusiness and industry.

The "integrated" vision of agrarian reform, however, demands a radical shift in state policies and resources *away* from the export-oriented agro-industrial sector, and towards the domestic-focused peasant sector. This vision of agrarian reform insists that peasant-oriented policies take center stage. There is little political will for this project in the current government, which is going in precisely the opposite direction. But the proposed law represents a political vision crafted by peasants and civil society, and potentially a roadmap for the "refoundation" of Honduras demanded by the national resistance movement (FNRP and LIBRE). A radical shift in political power will be necessary for the implementation of "integrated agrarian reform" as envisioned by Honduran peasants; whether and how this shift will occur remains to be seen.

15
CONCLUSION

For over a century, the fertile Atlantic coast of Honduras has been targeted for export agriculture at the expense of peasant food production, sparking the rise of militant peasant movements. These movements won important reforms in the 1960s, which placed land distribution at the center of national agricultural development for over two decades. The remote tropical settlement of Tocoa, in the heart of the Aguán Valley, became known in the 1970s as the "national capital of agrarian reform" (Macías 2011). Encouraged by government land grants and technical support for agriculture, peasants from around the country came to the Aguán in the hopes of a better life.

The neoliberal policies of the 1990s, however, rapidly reversed these gains leading to dramatic increases in land concentration, rural poverty, out-migration and dependence on the global market for food. The 1992 Agrarian Modernization Law embodied the emerging neoliberal consensus centered on the World Bank's discourse of "market-led agrarian reform." This approach entailed the privatization of land, transforming it from a collective good into a commodity that could be bought and sold. Over time, neoliberal agrarian reform proved to be highly regressive: instead of promoting the transfer of land to the poor, the reforms did the opposite. By bringing peasant lands into the free market—under economic conditions hostile to peasant producers—neoliberal land policies led to mass displacement, unemployment and outmigration. Elites like Miguel Facussé gained handsomely by buying land cheaply from peasants in economic distress. Thousands of landless workers immigrated to the United States in search of work or poured into precarious jobs in manufacturing zones as a result.

The colossal transfer of land away from the peasantry into the hands of a few powerful families might logically be seen as a "failure" of market-led agrarian reform, as promoted by USAID and the World Bank. As Holt-Giménez (2007) points out, however, one must look beyond these institutions' stated missions to "reduce poverty" to their core function, which is to create enabling conditions for capital accumulation: "A market-based land reform project may be an agrarian failure for the peasantry, yet still be quite successful in terms of helping restructure the social and economic institutions in a country's hinterlands in favor of agribusiness, tourism, or extractive industries, for example."

Indeed, neoliberal policies—including, but not limited to, land privatization—helped to restructure northern Honduras in favor of elite-controlled sectors, namely manufacturing, palm oil and tourism. In turn, elites gained the "incredible ability not only to amass large personal fortunes but to exercise a controlling power over large segments of the economy [conferring] on these few individuals immense economic power to influence political processes" (Harvey 2005, 34). Grabbing land was (and is) part of a larger class project of "grabbing power."

These agro-industrial oligarchs continue to receive support from international financial institutions like the World Bank, IDB and other sources of financing—such as the UN Clean Development Mechanism—that allow corporations to capture value in the new "green" economy. What's more, they are bolstered by an increasingly militarized public and private security apparatus that is magnified by the US War on Drugs. Since the 2009 coup, the peasants, indigenous communities and Garifuna people of northern Honduras face a mounting hostility to their very existence on the land that is tantamount to all-out war.

BOX 10. NORTH-SOUTH SOLIDARITY AND ACTIVIST RESEARCH

Citizens of the Global North can play an important role in supporting community-based struggles for land and justice in Honduras. The most urgent task is to apply pressure on government officials and institutions to demand the suspension of security aid and of spending on a failed War on Drugs that lines the pockets of elites while terrorizing rural communities. These solidarity efforts have already yielded positive results. In March 2011, 94 members of the US House of Representatives signed a letter calling for the suspension of police and military aid to Honduras, especially in light of the human rights abuses in the Aguán. As Frank (2012) puts it, "Congress didn't just suddenly grow a spine by itself, of course. Activists in the Honduras Solidarity Network and their allies have hammered away for almost three years to build support at the grassroots level and translate it into power in Washington—and Honduras."

Solidarity activists can support social movements through scholarship, art and media that legitimize movements for genuine democracy and redistributive justice. Examples of such efforts include community radio stations; cultural groups like Artists in Resistance; blogs, list servs and social media sites controlled by movements and activists; action alerts by international allies; and international independent media. The importance of these forms of knowledge production and dissemination is underscored by the extreme repression against Honduran media workers who dare to oppose the coup or highlight the voices of social movements. At the time of this writing, 22 Honduran journalists have been murdered since the 2009 coup for daring to break the silence of elite-managed censorship (UNESCO 2012). This makes the work of international solidarity media that much more vital.

Pressure from international observers can help to protect the lives of Aguán peasants, especially high profile movement leaders, who are routinely threatened and detained. On January 8, 2011, peasant activist Juan Chinchilla, a representative of MUCA and Youth in Resistance, was kidnapped and tortured for 48 hours. An international campaign immediately went into effect, with human rights activists from around the world demanding his immediate release. Chinchilla comments that his captors "were monitoring the news on the internet and radio":

> I believe that all of this pressure helped so that something worse did not happen. I am infinitely grateful to all of the people and organizations— national and international—that mobilized; and also the media that denounced my kidnapping. (Trucchi 2011)

Responding to "action alerts" by solidarity organizations shows Honduran movements that they are not alone; it shows local authorities (who often act with impunity) that their actions are being scrutinized; and it shows North American officials that citizens are paying attention to their governments' inaction, if not complicity, regarding political repression. For those with more time and resources, joining a human rights fact-finding mission or solidarity delegation can also be useful by gathering first-hand accounts of peasant struggles to break the media stonewall, and accompanying activists during moments of heightened possibility of repression (demonstrations, evictions, elections, etc.). A number of North-based solidarity groups—e.g. Alliance for Global Justice, Friendship Office of the Americas, Rights Action, SOA Watch, Witness for Peace—sponsor delegations and long-term accompaniment opportunities in partnership with Honduran groups.

It is also important to recognize that the mainstream media, often controlled by elite interests in both the North and South, plays an important role in criminalizing grassroots movements. Like poor communities fighting for justice around the world, Honduran movements endure negative media portrayals that depict their struggles as crime, terrorism, gang activity or drug violence. These depictions, insofar as they are not questioned or refuted, fuel justifications for repression, incarceration and increased security budgets for waging war on peasants. The elite-controlled Honduran media regularly lends credence to the unfounded accusations of rich landowners, who describe peasant communities as violent, armed insurgencies funded by outsiders.[101]

Honduras is an under-studied and poorly understood country relative to most of Latin America. This book has attempted to lay out the context of rural development and changing power relations in northern Honduras, but it is by no means a comprehensive or final analysis. Further research is needed, especially on the relationship between political power and control over land and resources. The country's strategic importance to the United States in the context of the War on Drugs and broader geopolitical interests in the region warrant greater (and urgent) analysis, especially considering the situation of rapidly escalating violence and insecurity.

With respect to the emerging scholarship on "land grabbing," this book has suggested that the new land grabs in Honduras (and elsewhere) be viewed as an outgrowth of the neoliberal policies that led to dramatic concentrations of wealth and political power. At the same time, the social movements briefly profiled in these pages are not only reacting to current or recent land grabs. Rather, they are rooted in historic grassroots opposition to the neoliberal project and its erosion of community power. For activist researchers in both the North and the South, this is a fertile avenue for impactful scholarship.

Grabbing Power Back

In the 1990s, the future of redistributive agrarian reform looked bleak. While "democratization" in many countries of the Global South opened a space for social movements to make political demands, neoliberal restructuring decreased government accountability to civil society. Thus, the state came to "function as an organizational tool for market expansion, and less a vehicle for representative democracy or resource distribution" (Courville and Patel 2006, 8). Ironically, the "golden age" of agrarian reform in Honduras occurred under military dictatorship in the 1960s and 70s, while the dismantling of its achievements occurred *after* the return to civilian rule and electoral democracy in the 1980s. This reality has not been lost on Hondurans who, especially since the post-coup "election" of Porfirio Lobo, increasingly question the true meaning of democracy.

Around the world, the re-concentration of land in favor of elites, accompanied by the reduced accountability of the state to social demands, led to a "phenomenal rise in land occupations and reclamations—land reform from below—being carried by a new generation of sophisticated social movements" (Rosset 2011, 24). For example:

> In Indonesia, some 1 million hectares of land have been occupied by landless peasants since the end of the Suharto dictatorship (…) In Brazil, according to the Landless Workers' Movement (MST), by 2002 some 8 million hectares of land have been occupied and settled by some 1 million people newly engaged in farming. Other countries with escalating land occupations include Paraguay, Bolivia, Nicaragua, Argentina, Honduras, Guatemala, Mexico, India, Thailand, South Africa, and others. (ibid.)

Thanks to grassroots movements, the global food crisis and the new wave of land grabs, the need for agrarian reform is back in the global spotlight. But the "new generation" of peasant

Members of the peasant movement MARCA on an occupied Aguán oil palm plantation (photo by Roger Harris)

movements—most prominently, but not exclusively, embodied by Vía Campesina—demands more than the state-led reforms of the past, which sought to limit peasant autonomy rather than enhance it. Aware of the limitations of past reforms, the new movements call for *integrated* reforms that democratize food, land and political power writ large. Increasingly, they demand policies that support the right of rural and working peoples everywhere to access, control and benefit from land, territory and resources—what Borras and Franco (2012) refer to as "land sovereignty."

In the Aguán, peasant movements remain rooted in historic struggles tied to the region's identity as part of the "reform sector," an identity created by the state-led agrarian reform and cooperativization programs of the 1970s. But neoliberal restructuring and the militarized response to peasant movements have radicalized the Aguán. The new movements have gone beyond traditional demands for land redistribution (though these remain central) to demands for a *large-scale project of counter-restructuring that restores political and economic power to local communities.* This project necessarily entails a transformation of state power, or "grabbing power back" from the small class of globalized elites who currently control the state. It requires broad-based alliances linking cooperatives, contract farmers, landless rural and urban workers, and broad sectors of civil society, nationally and internationally. The irony of the 2009 coup—which sought to further entrench the power of the agro-industrial oligarchy—is that it created precisely the right conditions for these alliances to take hold.

APPENDIX
DECLARATION OF THE INTERNATIONAL HUMAN RIGHTS OBSERVATORY OF AGUÁN[102]

We, the members of Honduran social movements, peasant organizations of Aguán, the National Front of Popular Resistance in Colón, and international human rights organizations who come together for the inauguration of the International Human Rights Observatory of Aguán jointly declare:

That the situation of constant violation of human rights against various communities in the department of Colón, on the Atlantic coast of Honduras, has intensified as the climate of terror, assassinations, persecution and repression of peasant groups in the region continues to escalate. Private security guards and mercenaries working for businessmen and powerful landowners including Miguel Facussé, Reinaldo Canales and René Morales as well as members of the judiciary continue to threaten the safety of human rights defenders in the region.

That these landowners, supported by the National Agrarian Institute, Ministry of Agriculture and Ministry of Security under president Porfirio Lobo are now operating a third wave of militarization (Xatruch II) in the Aguán, using conventional ground-war weapons such as helicopters and armed aircrafts ready for use.

Since the coup of June 28, 2009—and especially since December 9, 2009 when the agrarian conflict escalated—conditions in the Aguán have deteriorated in many ways, including:

a. **The criminalization of peasant movements for the right to land.** The Honduran Supreme Court abolished Decree Law 18 - 2008, which had promoted mediation between the state and landowners to resolve land disputes. This led to the evictions of thousands of families who had farmed these lands for many years but had not yet obtained clear titles. These evictions, many involving the removal of indigenous people from their ancestral lands, cleared the way for domestic and foreign capital to build "charter cities" in clear violation of national sovereignty. Media groups owned by members of the Honduran oligarchy have initiated a smear campaign against the Aguán peasant movements, alleging that peasants are organized in armed guerilla groups consisting of criminals, thieves and other delinquents. These media groups continue to spread misinformation, so that the international community will remain unaware of the evictions of innocent families in the Aguán.

b. Record numbers of assassinations of members of community organizations. Although 46 peasants have been killed in this agrarian conflict, the justice department has done nothing to identify the perpetrators of these crimes.

c. Violent raids on communities create a climate of terror. Three raids were carried out between June and November 2011 against the Peasant Movement of Rigores. In the first raid, the entire community was destroyed by burning homes, crops, schools and churches. Adults and children from Rigores have been kidnapped and tortured, physically and psychologically. Raids have also been carried out against the communities of Marañones, La Confianza, La Aurora and La Lempira. The raids are carried out by police, military, private guards and mercenaries, usually wearing ski masks. Colonel Espinal, the operations commander of Xatruch II, claims that the objective is the general "disarmament" of peasant communities.

d. Targeted shootings and assassinations in rural settlements. Guards, police, and military personnel hide in African palm plantations and fire live ammunition rounds on peasants and workers. Three members of the MARCA peasant movement, Catarino Efraín Lopez, José Luis Lemus and Ceferino Zelaya, were killed in the peasant settlement of Aurora. Residents of several settlements are afraid to leave their homes due to the constant threat of capture and assassination.

e. Kidnappings and forced disappearance of peasants. Francisco Pascual Lopez from Rigores was kidnapped and remains missing. Community members witnessed security guards open fire and carry his bloodied body into a palm plantation belonging to Miguel Facussé. Secundino Gómez and eighteen-year-old Olvin Gallegos were both kidnapped on May 29, 2011 and are still missing. Segundo Mendoza of the MARCA peasant movement was kidnapped on October 14, 2011 and later discovered in the morgue in the city of La Ceiba, with clear signs of assassination, his body missing a hand.[103] That same night another MARCA member, Carlos Alberto Hernández Ramos was taken to the police station in Sonaguera, beaten and tortured for 24 hours. He was released under threat of further torture if he revealed anything about what had happened.

f. Death threats and surveillance of peasant leaders. At least 30 peasant leaders, in addition to FNRP leaders and human rights defenders have received death threats and are continuously followed by armed men and vehicles without license plates.

g. Military operations near peasant settlements and "capture orders" against individuals. There are more than 300 arrest warrants or "capture orders" in the courts in Colón. These orders allow the military to detain a person for up to two hours. They often demand bribes from detainees and hold them until they pay. They claim to be searching for weapons and for foreign insurgents.

h. Continuous violation of signed agreements. The government continues to violate or fail to honor the agreements and conventions signed with peasant movements. Meanwhile, large landowners employ over two thousand armed men to protect their landholdings, waiting for the region to be "pacified."

Due to the severe threats against peasants in the Aguán, we pledge:
1. To defend the human rights of men, women and children living under constant harassment, repression and insecurity.
2. To be present during evictions, raids and military interventions, and stand with the victims as they assert their right to land.
3. To provide protection to those who are threatened, persecuted or repressed.

4. To provide support including medical care and legal assistance to those affected by the land conflict.
5. To denounce the human rights violations nationally and internationally and create mechanisms for immediate responses.
6. To bring legal action, through national and international judicial processes, against those who violate human rights in the region.

End the killing of peasants in Honduras! End human rights violations in the Aguán!

Tocoa, Colón, November 11, 2011

Signed:
MCA
MARCA
MUCA MARGEN IZQUIERDA
MUCA MARGEN DERECHA
MOVIMIENTO CAMPESINO RIGORES
EMPRESA CAMPESINA BUENOS AIRES
EMPRESA CAMPESINA ORICA
CENTRO JUVENIL HORIZONTES DE ESPERANZA
COPA
COPINH
OFRANEH
POPOL NAH TUN
FUNDACION SAN ALONSO RODRIGUEZ
ASOCIACION DE ABOGADOS POR LA JUSTICIA
COORDINACION FNRP-COLON
FIAN INTERNACIONAL
FIAN HONDURAS
RIGHTS ACTION
CICA

STAY INFORMED & GET INVOLVED

You can stay informed about developments in Honduras by consulting the following online resources. You can also make a tax-deductible donation to North America-based solidarity groups Rights Action and Alliance for Global Justice (AFGJ) (see below).

Online Resources:

MUCA: http://movimientomuca.blogspot.com

MCA: http://movimientocampesinodelaguan.blogspot.com

MUCA-MI: http://muca-mi.blogspot.com

MioAguan: http://mioaguan.blogspot.com/p/ingles.html

FNRP: www.resistenciahonduras.net

LIBRE: http://libertadyrefundacion.com

COPINH: www.copinh.org

COFADEH: www.cofadeh.org

Defensores en Línea (COFADEH media):
www.defensoresenlinea.com

OFRANEH: www.ofraneh.org/ofraneh/index.html

CODEMUH: http://codemuh.net

Honduras Resists (La Voz de los de Abajo):
http://hondurasresists.blogspot.com

Artists in Resistance: http://artistaresiste.blogspot.com

FIAN Honduras: www.fian.hn

Rights Action: www.rightsaction.org

AFGJ: www.afgj.org

Quotha (Adrienne Pine): www.quotha.net

Rel-Uita: www.rel-uita.org

Honduras Culture and Politics:
http://hondurasculturepolitics.blogspot.com

Vía Campesina: http://viacampesina.org/en

Vos el Soberano: http://voselsoberano.com

Donate to Rights Action:

With tax-charitable status in the USA and Canada, Rights Action funds community-controlled development, environmental, human rights and emergency-relief projects in Guatemala, Honduras, Chiapas and Oaxaca (Mexico) and El Salvador, and does education and activism work with North Americans to address global exploitation, repression, environmental destruction and racism. Rights Action sends funds directly to Honduran organizations, including organizations in the Aguán, for their work and for emergency responses including medical needs and expenses. Support this initiative by sending a check to Rights Action with "Aguán" in the memo line. Contributions are tax-deductible in the US and Canada. Funds will be sent directly to the peasant movements. Make check payable to "Rights Action" and mail to:

UNITED STATES: Box 50887, Washington DC, 20091-0887
CANADA: 552 - 351 Queen St. E, Toronto ON, M5A-1T8

CREDIT-CARD DONATIONS can be made
(anonymously): www.rightsaction.org
DONATIONS OF STOCK can be made
(anonymously): info@rightsaction.org

Donate to Alliance for Global Justice (AFGJ):

The mission of Alliance for Global Justice (AFGJ) is to achieve social change and economic justice by helping to build a stronger more unified grassroots movement. AFGJ supports locally-based grassroots organizing by sharing political analysis, mobilizing for direct action, monitoring the centers of corporate and government power, expanding channels of communication, and sharing skills and infrastructure. AFGJ supports the peasant movements of the Aguán by providing skilled accompaniment from North America to monitor human rights and accompany local movements to prevent abuses. To support this initiative, send a check payable to "AFGJ" with "Honduras Accompaniment" in the memo line. Mail to: Alliance for Global Justice, 1247 E St., SE, Washington, DC 20003. Or donate online at: https://afgj.org/afgj-donations

ACRONYMS

AHMUC – Association of Peasant Women of Honduras

AML – Agricultural Modernization Law

ANACH – National Association of Honduran Peasants

APROH – Association for the Progress of Honduras

CABEI – Central American Bank for Economic Integration

CARSI – Central American Regional Security Initiative

CDM – Clean Development Mechanism of the United Nations

CER – Certified Emission Reduction credit (or "carbon credit")

CICA – Collettivo Italia Centro America

CNTC – National Union of Peasant Workers

CODEMUH – Honduran Women's Collective

CODEL – Local Emergency Committee (after Hurricane Mitch)

CODETT – Committee to Defend the Land of Triunfo

COFADEH – Committee for Relatives of the Detained and Disappeared in Honduras

COHEP – Honduran Council of Private Enterprises

COPA – Coordinating Committee of Popular Organizations of Aguán

COPINH – Civic Council of Popular and Indigenous Organizations of Honduras

CREM – Regional Center for Military Training

EFB – empty (palm) fruit bunch

EPZ – Export Processing Zone

FENACH – National Federation of Honduran Peasants

FENAGH – National Federation of Farmers and Ranchers

FIAN – FoodFirst International Action Network

FNRP – National Front of Popular Resistance

FTF – Feed the Future (USAID initiative)

IACHR – Inter-American Commission on Human Rights

IDB – Inter-American Development Bank Group

IFC – International Finance Corporation of the World Bank

IHMA – National Agricultural Marketing Board

IMF – International Monetary Fund

INA – National Agrarian Institute

LIBRE – Freedom and Refoundation (political party)

MAO – Environmental Movement of Olancho

MARCA – Authentic Movement for the Revindication of Aguán Peasants

MBC – Mesoamerican Biological Corridor

MCA – Peasant Movement of Aguán

MUCA – Unified Movement of Aguán Peasants

NSD – national security doctrine

OFRANEH – Black (Garifuna) Fraternal Organization of Honduras

PME – palm methyl ester (biodiesel)

POME – palm oil mill effluent

RBD – refined, bleached and deodorized (palm oil)

RED – Special Development Region or "Charter City"

RSPO – Roundtable on Sustainable Palm Oil

SAP – structural adjustment program/policies

USAID – United States Agency for International Development

WWF – World Wildlife Fund

NOTES

1   e.g. FIAN, Food First, Friends of the Earth, GRAIN, Grassroots International, International Land Coalition, Oakland Institute, Oxfam, Transnational Institute, Vía Campesina and others.

2   This was the case in Paraguay, for example, where the concentration of land for export soy production appears to have consolidated elite power leading up to the June 22, 2012 overthrow (dubbed a "constitutional" or "parliamentary" coup) of president Fernando Lugo (see Dangl 2012).

3   This changed somewhat with the growth in commercial beef exports (and expansion of large ranches) in the 1950s and 60s, causing ecological degradation, hunger, displacement and outmigration in those regions (Boyer 1986; Howard-Borjas 1995). But the rural oligarchy still remained weak in Honduras compared to neighboring countries like El Salvador, where a few wealthy families made fortunes from coffee exports in the 19th century and moved on to control trade and banking (LaFeber 1984, 43).

4   The now-defunct APROH even submitted a proposal to president Reagan's Kissinger Commission advocating the military invasion of Nicaragua (Envío 1984).

5   Like many Latin American business and governing elites (often educated in US institutions like MIT or Texas A&M), Honduran elites see Miami is their preferred social and cultural hub. This was illustrated by US ambassador to Honduras Charles Ford (2008-2009) in a recent WikiLeaks cable in which he mocks ousted president Manuel Zelaya, saying, "Zelaya's view of a trip to the 'big city' means Tegucigalpa and not Miami or New Orleans." (Reported by anthropologist Adrienne Pine on her blog Quotha.net: "Wikileaks 08TEGUCIGALPA459: Ambassador Charles Ford on Zelaya" Dec. 10, 2010. Accessed August 2012. http://quotha.net/node/1432

6   It also raises the value of those lands, making their progressive redistribution *with compensation at market value* (as opposed to politically difficult forced expropriation) increasingly unaffordable for peasants and state agencies alike (at least without taking on tremendous debt burdens).

7   This phrase is borrowed from White et al. (2012) p. 635.

8   Due to mass layoffs by fruit companies following the strike, a labor force of 35,000 plantation workers in 1953 was reduced to 27,000 in 1955 and to 16,000 in 1959 (Nelson 2003: 7).

9   Following the 1954 general strike, the United States and Honduras signed a bilateral military assistance agreement whereby the US pledged to build up the Honduran military (in exchange for increased access to raw materials). Thus, despite US support for the reforms of president Villeda Morales, he was overthrown by a strengthened military in 1963. With continued grassroots pressure from the peasantry,

the ensuing military regimes continued the agrarian reform process (some say reluctantly) until the 1980s when organized peasant groups were increasingly targeted by the US-assisted counter-insurgency war.

10   Part of the Aguán Valley had been used by for banana production until the early 1930s, but the fruit companies abandoned the region due to the advance of Panama disease. Thirty years later, by the time of the agrarian reform, the lands had mostly reverted to forest (and to the state), with only a small population concentrated in a few towns (Jones 1990).

11   Heretofore, I refer to these peasant enterprises as "cooperatives" for the sake of simplicity, and because the word "enterprise" in English does not accurately represent the collective values inherent to the *empresa campesina*. In actuality, there are a number of different legal entities (e.g. *cooperativas, empresas campesinas, asociaciones de productores*, etc.) that comprise the "social sector" of the Honduran economy, as opposed to the "private" and the "public" (state-owned) sectors (see COHDESSE 2010). Thank you to Andrés León for pointing out the importance of noting this distinction.

12   Honduras kept a fixed exchange rate vis-à-vis the US dollar for over seven decades. Until February 1990, Honduran currency remained stable at around 2 lempiras per dollar. Between 1990 and late 1992, its value was fixed at around 5.4 lempiras per dollar and after 1992 it was allowed to fluctuate freely (Esquivel and Larrain 1999). Since 1992, the value of the lempira against the dollar has decreased steadily—with an average exchange rate of 6.5:1 in 1993, 14.4:1 in 1995 and 18.8:1 in 2005. (UN Data > International Financial Statistics > Exchange Rates: http://data.un.org/ Data retrieved Oct. 19, 2012)

13   Beans, maize, rice, sorghum, soy, cattle, poultry, poultry meat, pork, milk, eggs and beef (Thorpe 2002, 182 n37)

14   Zelaya's minimum wage law, passed in December 2008, raised the monthly minimum wage from US$158 to $289. Nevertheless, it did not apply to the country's EPZs, which constitute the majority of the country's manufacturing areas (Mejía 2009).

15   This "surplus population" is part of what Bernstein (2004) calls the "agrarian question of labor" created when people are displaced from agriculture and absorbed into manufacturing as low-wage labor. In most cases, where there is no industrial revolution generating new jobs for dispossessed peasants, urban migrants become part of expanding urban slums. As White et al. (2012) point out, "surplus population" here is "the result of capital accumulation and technical progress, which is 'surplus' (…) to capital's requirements for labor, resulting in low wages of the employed and pauperism of the un- and underemployed even in contexts of rapid economic development" (625).

16   Decree Law 31-92

17   For a discussion of different agrarian reform paradigms, see Rosset et al. 2006.

18   For example, Facussé is the uncle of former president Carlos Flores Facussé (1998-2002), whose family owns the major newspaper La Tribuna.

Flores Facussé's daughter Elizabeth "Lizzy" Flores was named Honduran ambassador to the United Nations in 2010 (she is also married to the agro-industrialist Freddy Násser). Miguel Facussé is also the uncle of congresswoman Marcía Facussé Andonie de Villeda and of Adolfo Facussé, president of the National Association of Industrialists (ANDI).

19 This class of agro-oligarchs, therefore, benefitted doubly from the indebtedness of the state: first, from the infrastructure financed by state debt, and second, from the adjustment policies implemented to restructure the debt.

20 While the Obama administration claimed to have cut all military ties with Honduras following the coup, the US army continued training Honduran officers at its training facility in Fort Benning, Georgia (formerly known as the US Army School of the Americas or SOA) (Hodge and Cooper 2009). A number of SOA graduates are linked to the Honduran coup, including Romeo Orlando Vásquez Velásquez, the general who overthrew Zelaya.

21 Honduras is Open for Business > Programa Nacional de Promoción de Inversiones   http://www.hondurasisopenforbusiness.com/programa.php (accessed February 2012)

22 Honduras is Open for Business > Productive Sectors http://www.hondurasopenforbusiness.com/en/projectlist.php?id=3 (accessed February 2012)

23 Zelaya's Liberal Party (PL), like the opposition National Party (PN), emerged at the turn of the twentieth century with close ties to the US fruit companies (the PN closely tied to United Fruit and the PL partisan to Cuyamel Fruit) (Barry 1991, 290). For over a century, the PN and PL have dominated the political scene, with little substantive difference in their stance on major issues.

24 The referendum actually asked Hondurans whether they wished to include a measure on the next ballot (the now-infamous *cuarta urna*) that would ask them to *vote again* on convening a new constituent assembly. This is far removed from the rumor, especially touted in the English-language media, that Zelaya was vying to remain "president for life." The drafting of a new constitution *might* have included provisions to extend presidential term limits—thin grounds for a military coup, to say the least. Further, it is highly unlikely a constitutional assembly would have finished the task of redrafting the constitution before Zelaya's presidential term expired in January 2010.

25 Less than a week after this story was published, on May 11, 2012, FAST units were involved in a massacre of innocent civilians in the indigenous Moskitia region in Northeast Honduras. The victims received multiple gunshots from high-caliber M-60 firearms, fired from a US helicopter manned by DEA agents and Honduran officers. Four people were killed: 28-year-old Juana Jackson (six months pregnant), 48-year-old Candelaria Pratt Nelson (five months pregnant), 14-year-old Hasked Brooks Wood, and 21-year-old Emerson Martínez Henríquez. At least four more were seriously injured (COFADEH 2012; McCain 2012).

26 Thank you to Karen Spring for helping to clarify the extremely complicated nature of US-Honduran military cooperation and investments.

27 Adelio Muñoz (Orica), personal communication. Aguán Valley, Honduras. January 11, 2012.

28 Daniel Gómez (MUCA), personal communication. Aguán Valley, Honduras. January 10, 2012.

29 Division General Venancio Cervantes was appointed Director of Migration and Immigration (he was assistant director of the Joint Chiefs of Staff at the time of the coup); Brigade General Manuel Enrique Cáceres was appointed Director of Civil Aeronautics; General Nelson Wily Mejía is now in charge of the Marine Mercantile Administration and General Romeo Vásquez Velásquez (Commander-in-Chief of the Armed Forces at the time of the coup) is now head of the Honduran Telecomunicaciones company Hondutel (FIDH 2011: 7, n.10).

30 An international human rights mission reported that media outlets were fabricating images by placing high caliber weapons on the bodies of murdered Aguán peasants for photographs, and then removing them (FIDH 2011: 27). This systematic criminalization of peasants contributes to a strong stigma, even causing peasants to be refused medical care in local hospitals (FIDH 2011: 27).

31 Anonymous peasants, personal communications, Aguán Valley, Honduras. June 2011 and January 2012.

32 Daniel Gómez (MUCA), personal communication, Tocoa, Aguán Valley, Honduras. January 10, 2012.

33 The win-win arguments put forth by the palm oil industry mirror those used to defend "responsible" land grabbing (dubbed "agricultural investment") (FAO 2009; World Bank 2010). Brazilian activist Giselle Henriques (2008) comments, "the specter of a hungry world is being used to push the agenda for industrial agriculture, but in reality, the majority of the land is used for producing animal feed and agrofuels, as well as land speculation, rather than food crops" (cited in McMichael 2012: 688, n. 11).

34 Quoted in Sarif, Edy. 2012. "Huge Opportunities in Palm Oil" The Star Online (Malaysia), March 7, 2012. http://biz.thestar.com.my/news/story.asp?file=/2012/3/7/business/10866837&sec=business (accessed July 2012)

35 Processed foods like candy bars, cake frosting, ice cream, coffee creamer, margarine, peanut butter, canned cream soups, sauces, snacks, baked goods and microwavable convenience foods all may contain palm oil (CSPI 2005: 6).

36 Fertilizer is the largest investment in oil palm production. Medium and large producers tend to apply a higher quantity of fertilizer than small producers, since they have more disposable income. Urea is the most widely used fertilizer, followed by superphosfate, potassium sulfate, potassium chloride, borax and magnesium sulfate (Sanders et al. 2006: 65).

37 The case of cotton is emblematic and has led to fierce battles in the WTO over subsidies to large US cotton producers, which depress

world prices and undermine smallholder producers, such as in West Africa (see Allston et al. 2007). For a general analysis of commodity production, trade liberalization and price impacts on family farmers, see Wise 2009.

38 Most Honduran palm oil exports are destined for Mexico (71%), followed by El Salvador (17%), the UK (8%), the Netherlands (2%) and Venezuela (2%) (SAG 2009: 8).

39 The latter deal was finalized in late 2009, on the cusp of a World Bank moratorium on palm oil lending instituted after widespread criticism of the industry's social and environmental impacts. The moratorium was lifted in April 2011 citing the importance of oil palm for economic growth and the Bank's commitment to improving social and environmental protections (Doering 2011).

40 The law, for instance, allows foreign firms to establish, acquire and dispose of businesses with no distinction from national firms, and encourages joint ventures with no minimum ownership for the Honduran partner.

41 See: http://www.usaid-acceso.org/index.aspx

42 In fact, this is part of a long history of US promotion of "non-traditional agricultural export crops" (NTAXs) in Central America. NTAXs include crops such as strawberries, celery, broccoli and lettuce—crops that have a high counter-seasonal demand in the US. In 1984, USAID set up the Honduran Agricultural Research Foundation (FHIA): a private, non-profit research institute focused on developing NTAX crops for US markets (Thorpe 2002, 89). The 1992 AML (articles 32 and 33) further supported this sector by eliminating taxes and permit requirements on NTAXs (95).

43 As of 2006, biodiesel produced from palm oil comprised only a 1% share of global biodiesel (compared to 84% for rapeseed oil, for instance). It is thought, however, that in the absence of high EU subsidies for domestic rapeseed producers, palm oil could become "by far the most competitive vegetable oil for the production of biodiesel" (Thoenes 2006: 5).

44 The stated goal of the Zelaya administration was to reach 200,000 hectares (494,210 acres) planted to oil palm in the country—through technical assistance and input subsidies to small and medium producers—by the end of the president's term in 2010 (Lefevre and Ramírez 2010). By 2011, it had reached approximately 135,000 hectares (333,592 acres) (USDA-FAS 2012b).

45 The eleven plants are owned by the following companies: Aceydesa (1), Dinant Corporation (2), Jaremar Corporation (4), Palcasa, Coapalma, Hondupalma and Salamá. The first four are private companies, while the last three are peasant-owned cooperatives created during the agrarian reform years (SAG 2009).

46 The peasant-owned palm oil plant with the largest capacity to produce biodiesel (Salamá) received its equipment through a donation of the Colombian government (Colombia is the largest palm oil producer

in the Americas). The Colombian government paid 70% and the Honduran government 30% of the cost of the equipment, valued at $100,000 USD (La Prensa 2009). The deal was made under the Zelaya administration and the plant inaugurated in March 2009, two months before his ouster.

47 SG Biofuels has since received millions in venture capital funding—including investment from the libertarian oil conglomerate Koch Industries—for expansion in Central America, Brazil and India (Herndon 2012).

48 According to a 2007 UNEP report, oil palm plantations are the leading cause of rainforest destruction in Malaysia and Indonesia creating one of the largest sources of greenhouse gas emissions in the world (Cited in Greenpeace 2007). In January 2012, the US Environmental Protections Agency (EPA) announced that, according to its calculations, palm oil biodiesel failed to meet emissions savings standards needed to qualify for the US renewable fuels program (Sun Daily 2012).

49 Adapted from: Shattuck, Annie. 2009. "Will Sustainability Certifications Work? A look at the Roundtable on Sustainable Biofuels" in *Agrofuels in the Americas*. Oakland: Food First Books, 118-132. (see original for references)

50 In response to criticism made in an Australian documentary titled "Conservation's Dirty Secrets" WWF made the following statement: "In April 2010, WWF signed a MOU with Exportadora del Atlántico, a subsidiary of Corporación Dinant. The MOU focused on improving their environmental performance… As a result of the program, better agricultural practices were implemented, specifically the production of compost to substitute the use of fertilizers… Late last year WWF became aware that there were allegations against the company concerning human rights abuses, specifically regarding a land dispute. This deeply concerned us, and at the beginning of December last year, we decided to suspend further work with the organisation pending further investigation." (WWF 2011)

51 Data retrieved from ECO2data Carbon Search Engine, search term: "Honduras" http://eco2data.com/ (accessed March 2012)

52 These mechanisms may also facilitate the "greening" of the maquila sector, which is beginning to receive carbon credits for converting from fossil fuels to palm-derived energy sources in its factories. This makes the maquila sector a large potential market for the oil palm industry. The (further) articulation of these two export-oriented industries plagued with human rights abuses is disconcerting, to say the least.

53 Njoi Residences are the investment of two Canadian couples (Paul and Lucia Todos, and Gino and Christina Santarossa). The project is described as "42 lots nestled within 34 acres of rainforest nature preserves along 800 feet of white sandy beach" See: http://www.njoitrujillo.com/ (accessed July 2012)

54 The comparatively smaller *southern* coast of Honduras has also been targeted by Miguel Facussé and other investors for "ecotourism" projects, particularly on the peninsula of Zácate Grande (La Tribuna 2012). These have been associated with forced evictions and other human rights abuses and have generated fierce resistance from local communities. The peasant movement of Zácate Grande issued a communiqué in January 2012 denouncing Facussé for grabbing land under the pretext of establishing a center for wildlife conservation (La Voz de Zácate Grande 2012). The English translation of the communiqué is available at Quotha.net: "Facussé's greenwashing operation in Zácate Grande" January 20, 2012. http://www.quotha.net/node/2073 (accessed August 2012)

55 Special thanks to Carla García and Karen Spring for sharing their knowledge and analysis of Garifuna land struggles and tourism investments.

56 For the IACHR, "'international human rights law imposes an obligation on the State to adopt special measures to guarantee the recognition of tribal peoples' rights, including the right to collectively own property.' The jurisprudence of the Inter-American Court of Human Rights in relation to the right to collective property applies not only to indigenous peoples, but also to tribal peoples who preserve their traditional ways of life based on a special link to their lands and territories." (IACHR 2010-2011: 282)

57 Coles (1988) describes "customary rights" as "rules which are transmitted from generation to generation, and which are socially recognized by local people" (cited in Jansen and Roquas 1998: 84). In other words, customary rights do not mean the absence of rules or property rights. In fact, customary tenure can work rather well at creating land claims that are respected by local people with few conflicts (ibid).

58 The law stipulates that foreigners may own land on the coasts, near national borders or on islands or cays, up to 3,000 square meters (approximately .75 acre). However, foreign investors or companies may purchase lands exceeding this amount with special permission from the Honduran Tourism Institute (IHT) (Meritas 2010).

59 Finley-Brook (2007) identifies three regional initiatives as the "tripartite vision" for the region's development: the Mesoamerican Biological Corridor; CAFTA; and Plan Puebla Panama (PPP) renamed the Mesoamerica Project in 2008. The goal of these projects is to combine privatization, liberalization, security and infrastructure (highways, ports, pipelines and electrical grids) to promote industrial development from Mexico in the north to Colombia in the south. The projects are primarily donor-driven, with key funding from the World Bank and IDB.

60 There are now 52 Garifuna land titles, all of which are of "full ownership" (*dominio pleno*) and communal, meaning that the land cannot be bought and sold and can only be passed through inheritance to members of the community (Brondo and Woods 2007: 8, n.5). While

this has been a significant achievement, titles do not include non-residential ancestral lands (ibid.) and titled lands are being purchased illegally by non-Garifuna investors (usually using a local intermediary) for tourism developments.

61 See OFRANEH. 2012. "El Banana Coast y la expulsión de los garífunas de la bahía de Trujillo" (video) http://www.youtube.com/watch?feature=player_embedded&v=6PhVwV-RvCc (accessed July 2012)

62 The six resisters were eventually pushed out. The community is now gone, the property fenced off, and construction is underway on either the cruise ship dock itself or other developments at the base of the future dock. With the area entirely fenced off it is difficult to tell exactly what they are doing. (Karen Spring, email communication, August 16, 2012)

63 The Los Micos "luxury eco-hotel" has an 18-hole golf course designed by golf legend Gary Player, 120 rooms, spa, restaurant, children's and teen clubs. One of the major foreign investors—along with a consortium of Honduran investors—is the US-based Trust Hospitality. The resort is slated for completion in summer 2013. See: Breaking Travel News. 2012. "Central America becoming focus for major hotel investment" May 22, 2012. http://www.breakingtravelnews.com/news/article/central-america-becoming-focus-for-major-hotel-investment/ (accessed July 2012)

64 See: Los Micos Beach and Golf Resort, http://www.losmicosresort.com/ (accessed July 2012)

65 Ironically, the park (formerly called Punta Sal) was renamed after Janet Kawas, an environmental activist who was murdered in 1995. Miguel Facussé, whose oil palm plantations were encroaching on the park, was implicated in the murder, but the case was never solved (Vos el Soberano 2011).

66 They have also suffered tremendous repression. The radio station Faluma Bimetu (*Coco Dulce*) in Triunfo de la Cruz—which broadcasts 70% of its programming in the Garifuna language—was burnt down in January 2010 after making anti-coup statements. It was soon rebuilt with support from international solidarity (Payne Roberts 2011). Additionally, numerous journalists and radio personalities from the urban-based, anti-coup radio stations (Radio Progreso, Radio Globo) have been killed or threatened. Since the coup, 22 reporters have been murdered in Honduras, making it one of the most dangerous countries in the world to be a journalist (UNESCO 2012).

67 Conference call with Garifuna leaders Carla García and Miriam Miranda (OFRANEH), August 29, 2012, sponsored by Agricultural Missions (www.agriculturalmissions.org)

68 "Food sovereignty is the right of peoples to healthy and culturally appropriate food produced through ecologically sound and sustainable methods, and their right to define their own food and agriculture systems. It puts those who produce, distribute and consume food at the

heart of food systems and policies rather than the demands of markets and corporations (…) Food sovereignty ensures that the rights to use and manage our lands, territories, waters, seeds, livestock and biodiversity are in the hands of those of us who produce food." (Vía Campesina 2007)

69   Maribel García (MUCA), personal communication, Aguán Valley, Honduras. January 14, 2012.

70   The other associations represented were the National Association of Honduran Peasants (ANACH), the National Union of Peasant Workers (CNTC) and the National Peasant Association (ACAN). (Ríos 2010)

71   A number of sources argue that cooperative lands might not have been sold, at least on such a large scale, had women had a greater voice in decision-making (Jeffrey 2001; Real News 2010; Vamos al Grano 2012). The lack of women's control over land decisions is, in part, a legacy of the highly gendered agrarian reform of the 1970s in which only 3.8% of the beneficiaries were women (CESPAD 2011). One woman peasant interviewed by the Real News (2010) commented, "I deeply regret that some bad Hondurans thought it was a good idea to sell the land. Unfortunately, the women weren't even consulted." In the new Aguán movements, one slogan of organized peasant women goes: *Con la mujer en la casa… la reforma agraria se atrasa!* (With women in the house… agrarian reform is delayed).

72   Calculated from data in Ríos (2010) and FIAN et al. (2011).

73   A statement by Facussé's Dinant Corporation, which contracted the security personnel to guard the plantation, claimed the guards had "shot in self-defense, as they were being attacked by invaders with high caliber weapons" (FIAN et al. 2011: n.41). The guards sustained no injuries.

74   Various MCA members, personal communication, Guadalupe Carney, Aguán Valley, January 12, 2012.

75   Claudia Ruíz (COPA), personal communication, Tocoa, Aguán Valley, Honduras. January 8, 2012.

76   Tyler Shipley is a researcher and activist based in Toronto, Canada. For a more detailed discussion of recent political trends in Honduras, see: "Left International Solidarity in Post-Coup Honduras" *Upside Down World*, Sept. 26, 2012. http://upsidedownworld.org/main/honduras-archives-46/3881-left-international-solidarity-in-post-coup-honduras

77   Zelaya returned to Honduras following the Cartagena Accords, signed in May 2011 in Cartegena, Colombia, mediated by the Colombian and Venezuelan governments. The accords opened the door to Honduras' re-entry in the Organization of American States (OAS).

78   Luis Alonzo Ortíz and Constantino Morales on July 16th and Julián Alvarenga (father of seven) on July 23rd

79   Claudia Ruíz (COPA), personal communication, Tocoa, Aguán Valley, Honduras. January 8, 2012

80   Due to MUCA's staunch refusal to sell palm fruit to Miguel Facussé (Jorge Mejía, MUCA member, personal communication, January 8,

2012, Tocoa, HN) the most recent agreement, signed June 1, 2012, stipulates that the cooperatives sell palm fruit to the peasant-owned Salamá and Hondupalma processing plants (La Tribuna 2012b).

81   On the challenges of building transnational agrarian movements, see Boyer 2010; DesMarais 2007; Edelman 2008; and Holt-Giménez 2010.

82   Wilfredo Paz (Observatory Spokesperson), personal communication, Tocoa, Aguán Valley, Honduras, January 10, 2012.

83   Quoted in Trucchi, Giorgio. 2010. "De Nuevo Corre Sangre en el Bajo Aguán" AlbaSud, November 23, 2010.

84   Altieri (1999) indicates that intensive peasant agriculture can be far more productive per unit of labor, even with little or no agrochemical use. On a typical highland Mayan farm, a single hectare of land can yield enough maize calories to feed a family of 5 to 7 people (199).

85   Trucchi, Giorgio. 2010. "De Nuevo Corre Sangre en el Bajo Aguán" AlbaSud, November 23, 2010. Author's translation.

86   Unless otherwise cited, all information from this chapter comes from author interviews with Salamá members, conducted at the Salamá processing plant and in the community of Suyapa, January 11, 2012

87   Salamá has not yet produced biodiesel on the donated equipment. As mentioned in the above chapter on agrofuels, none of the Aguán palm oil plants currently produce significant amounts of biodiesel. This is because of the high price of palm oil as an edible oil and the relatively low cost of government-subsidized gasoline. Because of these factors, PME biodiesel has rarely been price-competitive with fossil fuels in Honduras.

88   Jesse Freeston (investigative journalist for the Real News Network and director of the forthcoming documentary film Resistencia), email communication, May 17, 2012.

89   "Proyección Social de Hondupalma" Hondupalma.com, accessed May 2012. http://hondupalmahn.com/index.php?option=com_cont ent&view=article&id=78&Itemid=62

90   Jesse Freeston, email communication, May 17, 2012

91   Prieta cooperative president Rigoberto Fúnes and treasurer Freddy González Castro were both killed in February 2011 after fifteen high caliber bullets were fired into their truck (CRLN 2011). A few months later, in July 2011, Coapalma president Carlos Maradiaga was shot and killed in broad daylight, by two assailants on a motorcycle in La Ceiba (El Heraldo 2011d). Fúnes' replacement as president of Prieta (and González Castro's brother), Germán Castro, was also gunned down in September 2011, an attack that killed his wife Miriam Emelda Fiallo and left Castro paralyzed from the waist down (CRLN 2011). Castro is now living in exile with a bullet lodged in his spinal cord, hoping to get a visa to Cuba to have it removed (Jesse Freeston, email communication, May 17, 2012).

92   For his radical views on social change, Father Carney's Honduran citizenship was revoked in 1979 at which point he relocated to a parish in Nicaragua to work with peasants in the first years of the Sandinista

government. He was disappeared in 1983 after re-entering Honduras with a guerrilla group and was presumably executed by the military. Conflicting accounts suggest he may have starved to death, or been tortured and thrown alive from a helicopter over the rainforest (Acker 1988; May I Speak Freely? 2008). His body was never found.

93 Eduardo Flores (CNTC), Personal communication, Aguán Valley, Honduras, July 3, 2011.

94 Lyrics adapted and translated by the author. Original lyrics obtained from the Facebook page of Artists in Resistence: http://www.facebook.com/pages/ARTISTAS-en-RESISTENCIA/308660938708 (accessed June 2012); The song can be heard at Goear.com: http://www.goear.com/listen.php?v=dee27ec (accessed June 2012)

95 Jorge Mejía (MUCA), personal communication, Tocoa, Aguán Valley, Honduras, January 8, 2012.

96 Jorge Mejía (MUCA), personal communication, Tocoa, Aguán Valley, Honduras, January 8, 2012.

97 Jorge Mejía (MUCA), personal communication, Tocoa, Aguán Valley, Honduras, January 8, 2012.

98 Because of highly repressive conditions, MUCA representatives were not able to obtain visas to attend the awards ceremony in New York City, officiated by United Nations Special Rapporteur on the Right to Food, Olivier de Shutter. MUCA's Secretary General Yoni Rivas and Spokesperson Vitalino Álvarez were both beaten and detained, along with 25 other men and women, on August 21, 2012 while protesting peacefully outside the Supreme Court in Tegucigalpa. One of the 27 people arrested that day, human rights lawyer Antonio Trejo Cabrera was subsequently murdered by an unknown gunman while attending a friend's wedding in Tegucigalpa on September 22, 2012. Trejo had represented members of MARCA and MUCA in a number of legal cases.

99 Jorge Mejía (MUCA), personal communication, Tocoa, Aguán Valley, Honduras, January 8, 2012

100 Adelio Muñoz (Orica), personal communication. Aguán Valley, Honduras, January 11, 2012.

101 For example, an article in the prominent newspaper El Heraldo (2010b), owned by the powerful businessman Jorge Canahuati Larach, stated:

> The president of the National Association of Industrialists (ANDI), Adolfo Facussé, confirmed that he possessed detailed information revealing that a "replica" of the Colombian Armed Revolutionary Forces (FARC) was being formed in the Aguán. He explained that these people were taking advantage of the agrarian conflict in northern Honduras and receiving training from Nicaraguan elements. "They are forming a well-armed guerrilla force, encouraged by armed fighters in Nicaragua whose objective is to imitate the Colombian FARC," he denounced. He added that these movements are financed by

"friends" of Honduras in Venezuela and other places. The industrial leader expressed worry that "part of the Honduran territory is being occupied by guerrilla forces associated with drug traffickers." (author's translation)

These allegations were reported by El Heraldo despite the lack of any credible investigation or evidence, and without quoting peasant leaders or experts on the region who might refute these claims.

102 Translated and abridged by the author. Original Spanish version available at: http://muca-mi.blogspot.com/2011/11/11-de-noviembre-2011-declaracion-del.html

103 According to human rights activist Annie Bird (2012), "this is understood to mean that hit men used his hand to collect a reward."

REFERENCES

Acker, Alison. 1988. *Honduras: The Making of a Banana Republic.* Boston: South End Press.

AenR. 2010. "Guía Rápida de AenR Para el Boicot a Facussé" Artistas en Resistencia, December 3, 2010. Accessed June 2012. http://artistaresiste. blogspot.com/2010/12/guia-rapida-de-aenr-para-el-boicot.html

Alonso-Fradejas, Alberto. 2012. "Land Control-Grabbing in Guatemala: The political economy of contemporary agrarian change" Special issue of *The Canadian Journal of Development Studies* 33 (forthcoming).

Alston, Julien M., Daniel A. Sumner and Henrich Brunke. 2007. *Impacts of reduction of US cotton subsidies on West African cotton producers.* Washington, DC: Oxfam America.

Altieri, Miguel. 1999. "Applying Agroecology to Enhance the Productivity of Peasant Farming Systems in Latin America" *Environment, Development and Sustainability* 1: 197–217.

Amin, Samir. 2011. "Food Sovereignty: A Struggle for Convergence in Diversity" *Food Movements Unite!* Ed. Eric Holt-Giménez. Oakland: Food First Books.

Anderson, Mark. 2007. "When Afro Becomes (like) Indigenous: Garifuna and Afro-Indigenous Politics in Honduras" *Journal of Latin American and Caribbean Anthropology* 12, no. 2: 384–413.

Anseeuw, Ward, Liz Alden Wily, Lorenzo Cotula and Michael Taylor. 2012. "Land Rights and the Rush to Land" International Land Coalition, January 2012. Accessed February 2012. http://www.landcoalition.org/ sites/default/files/publication/1205/ILC%20GSR%20report_ENG.pdf

Appalasami, S. and R.J. de Vries. 1990. "The Future of Palm Oil in Oleochemicals" *Palm Oil Developments* 14, no. 3.

Ávila, José Francisco. 2006. *Historia de la Titulación de Tierras Garífuna en Honduras.* Providence, RI: Milenio Associates.

Barnes, Grenville and Gerald Riverstone. 2008. *Exploring vulnerability and resilience in land tenure systems after hurricanes Mitch and Ivan.* University of Florida. Unpublished manuscript.

Barry, Tom with Kent Norsworthy. 1991. "Honduras" *Central America Inside Out.* NY: Grove Press.

Biofuel-Watch. 2011. "Palm oil in the Aguan Valley, Honduras: CDM, bio-diesel and murders" Sept. 4, 2011. Accessed September 2011. http:// www.biofuelwatch.org.uk/2011/palm-oil-in-the-aguan-valley-honduras-cdm-biodiesel-and-murders/

Bird, Annie. 2011. "A Biofuels Ambassador: Obama names new ambassador to Honduras" Resistencia Honduras, April 21, 2011. Accessed April 2012. http://www.resistenciahonduras.net/index.php?option=com_content &view=article&id=2691:a-bio-fuels-ambassador-obama-names -new-ambassador-to-honduras&catid=101:news&Itemid=349

_____2012. "Repression is the 'Negotiation Strategy'" Rights Action, March 2, 2012. Accessed March 2012. http://www.rightsaction.org/

action-content/repression-negotiation-strategy-rudy-hernandez-ille-gally-detained-aguan-human-rights

Bolpress. 2011. "Raíces Históricas de la Fortuna de Miguel Facussé Barjum," June 4, 2011. Accessed January 2012. http://www.bolpress.com/art.php?Cod=2011060412

Borras, Saturnino M., Jennifer C. Franco, Sergion Gómez, Cristóbal Kay and Max Spoor. 2012. "Land Grabbing in Latin America and the Caribbean" *The Journal of Peasant Studies* 39, No. 3-4 (July-October): 845-872.

Boyer, Jefferson. 1986. "Capitalism, Campesinos and Calories In Southern Honduras" *Urban Anthropology and Studies of Cultural Systems and World Economic Development* 15, No. 1/2 (Spring/Summer): 3-24.

———— 2010. "Food security, food sovereignty, and local challenges for transnational agrarian movements: the Honduran case" *The Journal of Peasant Studies* 37, No. 2 (April): 319-351.

Boyer, Jeff and Aaron Pell. 1999. "Mitch in Honduras: A Disaster Waiting to Happen" NACLA, Vol. XXXIII, No. 2 (September/October).

Brondo, Keri Vacanti and Laura Woods. 2007. "Garifuna Land Rights and Ecotourism as Economic Development in Honduras' Cayos Cochinos Marine Protected Area" *Ecological and Environmental Anthropology* 3, No. 1.

Brondo, Keri Vacanti and Natalie Brown. 2011. "Neoliberal conservation, garifuna territorial rights and resource management in the cayos cochinos marine protected area" *Conservation and Society* 9, No. 2: 91-105.

Carrere, Ricardo. 2006. "Oil Palm: The Expansion of Another Destructive Monoculture" *Oil Palm from Cosmetics to Biodiesel, Colonization Lives On.* World Rainforest Movement, September 2006.

CCARC. 2002. *Organizaciones Indígenas y Negras en Centroamérica: Sus Luchas por Reconocimiento y Recursos.* Austin, TX: Caribbean Central American Research Council (CCARC).

CEJIL. 2009. "Gobierno de facto en Honduras debe cesar aplicación de toque de queda illegal" Center for Justice and International Law (CEJIL). Accessed January 2012. http://cejil.org/comunicados/gobierno-de-facto-en-honduras-debe-cesar-aplicacion-de-toque-de-queda-ilegal

CESPAD. 2011. "El MUCA margen derecha y la lucha campesina por la tierra en el Bajo Aguán" Centro de Estudios para la Democracia. Accessed April 2012. http://cespad.org/documentos/investigaciones/Estudio%20de%20casoMUCA%20AGUAN.pdf

Clay, Jason. 2004. *World Agriculture and the Environment: A Commodity by Commodity Guide to Impacts and Practices.* Washington DC: Island Press.

COHDESSE. 2010. "Documento Ilustrativo de la Economía Social en Honduras" Consejo Hondureño del Sector Social de la Economía. February 2010. Accessed October 2012. Available at: http://cohdesse.org/ley.php

COHEP. 2009. "Comunicado de Prensa COHEP 29 de Junio 2009." Accessed July 2012. Available at: http://www.cohep.com/noticias.html

Cotula, Lorenzo. 2012. "The International Political Economy of the Global Land Rush: A critical appraisal of trends, scale, geography and drivers" *The Journal of Peasant Studies*, 39, No. 3-4 (July-October): 649-680.

CSPI. 2005. "Cruel Oil: How Palm Oil Harms Health, Rainfoerst and Wildlife" Washington, DC: Center for Science in the Public Interest (CSPI), May 2005. Accessed May 2012. www.cspinet.org/palm/ PalmOilReport.pdf

Chopra, Mickey. 2002. "Globalization and Food: Implications for the Promotion of 'Healthy' Diets" *Globalization, Diets and Noncommunicable Diseases.* World Health Organization (WHO).

COCOCH. n.d. "Reforma Agraria, Agricultura y Medio Rural en Honduras: La agenda pendiente del sector campesino." Available at: http://www. scribd.com/doc/65349536/Reforma-Agraria-en-Honduras

COFADEH. 2009. "Violaciones a Derechos Humanos en el Marco del Golpe de Estado en Honduras: Cifras y Rostros de la Represión" Tegucigalpa: Comité de Familiares de Detenidos Desaparecidos en Honudras (COFADEH), October 22, 2009. Accessed January 2012. www.cofadeh.org/html/documentos/segundo_informe_situacionl_ resumen_violaciones_ddhh_golpe_estado.pdf

_____ 2012. "Informe Preliminar de Verificación Caso Ahuas, 11 de mayo de 2012" Report from COFADEH fact-finding mission to Ahuas and Puerto Lempira, Department of Gracias a Dios, May 20-24, 2012. Accessed July 2012. Available at: https://www.box.com/s/822eceea1aa08c550e44

Constance, Paul. 2008. "Interview: Private capital drives a green energy boom" IDBAmérica, April. Accessed March 2012. http://www.iadb.org/ idbamerica/index.cfm?thisid=4573

Courville, Michael and Raj Patel. 2006. "The Resurgence of Agrarian Reform in the Twenty-First Century" *Promised Land: Competing Visions of Agrarian Reform.* Oakland: Food First Books.

CRLN. 2011. "Politically Related Killings in Honduras Under President 'Pepe' Lobo" Chicago Religious Leadership Network on Latin America, November 12, 2011. Accessed May 2012. http://www.crln.org/ assassinations_in_Honduras

DanChurchAid. 2011. *Stolen Land Stolen Future: A report on land grabbing in Cambodia and Honduras.* Copenhagen, Denmark.

Dangl, Benjamin. 2012. "A Coup Over Land: The Resource War Behind Paraguay's Crisis" *Upside Down World,* July 16, 2012. Accessed August 2012. http://upsidedownworld.org/main/paraguay-archives-44/3758-a-coup-over-land-the-resource-war-behind-paraguays-crisis

Defensores en Línea. 2009. "Atentan contra dirigente popular de Tocoa" June 24, 2009. Accessed June 2012. http://www.defensoresenlinea.com/cms/ index.php?view=article&catid=42%3Aseg-y-jus&id=246%3Aatentan-contra-dirigente-popular-de-tocoa&option=com_content&Itemid=159

De Fontenay, C. 1999. *Institutions, Market Power and the Big Push: The Case of Agro-Exports in Northern Honduras.* Australia: University of New South Wales.

De Hoyos, Rafael E., Maurizio Bussolo and Oscar Nunez. 2008. "Can Maquila Booms Reduce Poverty? Evidence From Honduras" World Bank Policy Research Working Paper 4789. Washington, DC.: World Bank.

Deininger, Klaus and Derek Byerlee. 2011. "The Rise of Large Farms in Land Abundant Countries: Do They Have A Future?" World Bank Policy Research Working Paper 5588. Washington, DC.: World Bank.

Desmarais, Annette Aurélie. 2007. *La Vía Campesina: Globalization and the Power of Peasants.* Halifax: Fernwood Publishing.

Doering, Christopher. 2011. "World Bank lifts 18-month palm oil moratorium" Reuters, April 2, 2011. Accessed May 2012. http://in.reuters.com/article/2011/04/01/idINIndia-56064820110401

Eco2data. 2012. "Lean Biogas recovery from Palm Oil Mill Effluent (POME) ponds and biogas /biomass utilisation at Exportadora del Atlántico, Lean/Honduras" Eco2data.com. Last updated June 17, 2012. Accessed June 2012. http://eco2data.com/project/Lean-Biogas-recovery-from-Palm-Oil-Mill-Effluent-POME-ponds-and-biogas--biomass-utilisation-at-Exportadora-del-Atlntico-LeanHonduras-50117#tab_projectGeneral

Economist. 2011. "Honduras Shrugged" December 10, 2011. Accessed July 2012. http://www.economist.com/node/21541391

Edelman, Marc. 2008. "Transnational Organizing in Agrarian Central America: Histories, Challenges, Prospects" *Journal of Agrarian Change* 8, No. 2-3 (April): 229-257.

Eide, Asbjorn. 2009. "The Right to Food and the Impact of Liquid Biofuels" Rome: Food and Agriculture Organization (FAO). Accessed September 2011. http://www.fao.org/righttofood/publi08/Right_to_Food_and_Biofuels.pdf

El Ceibeño. 2012. "Terminal de cruceros en Trujillo estará lista en Octubre 2012" January 6, 2012. Accessed March 2012. http://www.elceibeno.hn/litoral/2012/01/en-octubre-estara-lista-terminal-de-cruceros/

El Heraldo. 2009a. "Cohep respalda gobierno de Micheletti" June 29, 2009. Accessed July 2012. http://archivo.elheraldo.hn/Al%20Frente/listado-nota/Ediciones/2009/06/30/Noticias/Cohep-respalda-gobierno-de-Micheletti

_____ 2009b. "Palmeros de Honduras negocian pago de deuda con Banadesa" July 1, 2009. Accessed March 2012. http://archivo.elheraldo.hn/Ediciones/2009/01/08/Noticias/Palmeros-de-Honduras-negocian-pago-de-deuda-con-Banadesa?utm_source=feedburner&utm_medium=feed&utm_campaign=Feed%253A+elheraldo_economia+%2528El+Heraldo+-+Economia%2529

_____ 2010a. "Se reaviva conflicto de tierras en Honduras" November 16, 2010. Accessed June 2012. http://archivo.elheraldo.hn/Ediciones/2010/11/17/Noticias/Se-reaviva-conflicto-de-tierras-en-Honduras

_____ 2010b. "En Honduras se forma réplica de las FARC, dice Adolfo Facussé" October 20, 2010. Accessed August 2012. http://archivo.elheraldo.hn/Ediciones/2010/10/20/Noticias/En-Honduras-se-forma-replica-de-las-FARC-dice-Adolfo-Facusse

_____ 2011a. "Tegucigalpa tendrá mall más grande de la region" March 30, 2011. Accessed August 2012. http://archivo.elheraldo.hn/Ediciones/2011/03/31/Noticias/Tegucigalpa-tendra-mall-mas-grande-de-la-region

_____2011b. "Cultivo de palma africana es solución para crisis petrolera" Reprinted by *Noticias de Energía*. April 15, 2011. Accessed May 2012. http://eeyer.wordpress.com/2011/04/15/cultivo-de-palma-africana-es-solucion-para-crisis-petrolera/

_____2011c. "Primera ciudad modelo se construirá en Trujillo" June 27, 2011. Accessed July 2012. http://archivo.elheraldo.hn/Ediciones/2011/06/28/Noticias/Primera-ciudad-modelo-se-construira-en-Trujillo

_____2011d. "Matan al presidente de Coalpalma" July 25, 2011. Accessed May 2012. http://archivo.elheraldo.hn/Ediciones/2011/07/26/Noticias/Matan-al-presidente-de-Coalpalma

_____2011e. "Desalojan a chortís de Copán Ruinas" December 15, 2011. Accessed June 2012. http://www.elheraldo.hn/Secciones-Principales/Pais/Desalojan-a-chortis-de-Copan-Ruinas

Elliott, Lauren. 2012. "Our Hope is in Our Struggle – Reclaiming Land and Life in Honduras" *Other Worlds*, April 27, 2012. Accessed May 2012. http://www.otherworldsarepossible.org/other-worlds/birthing-justice-our-hope-our-struggle-reclaiming-land-and-life-honduras

Emanuelsson, Dick. 2010. "Honduras: Los campesinos del Bajo Aguán: ¡Queremos reforma agraria ya!" Kaos en la Red, March 20, 2010. Accessed August 2012. http://old.kaosenlared.net/noticia/honduras-campesinos-bajo-aguan-queremos-reforma-agraria-ya

Envío. 1984. "Honduras: Militarized and Denationalized" *Revista Envío*, No. 35, May. Accessed August 2012. www.envio.org.ni/articulo/3914

_____ 1997. "Honduras: Popular Pressure in a Sea of Violence" *Revista Envío*, No. 192, July. Accessed July 2012. www.envio.org.ni/articulo/2028

_____ 2000. "After Hurricane Mitch: An Untold Story" *Revista Envío*, No. 226, May. Accessed August 2012. www.envio.org.ni/articulo/1421

Esquivel, Gerardo and Felipe Larrain. 1999. "Currency Crises: Is Central America Different?" Center for International Development at Harvard University. CID Working Paper No. 26, September.

Euraque, Darío A. 1996. *Reinterpreting the Banana Republic: Region & State in Honduras, 1870-1972*. Chapel Hill and London: University of North Carolina Press.

Fairhead, James, Melissa Leach and Ian Scoones. 2012. "Green Grabbing: A new appropriation of nature?" *The Journal of Peasant Studies* 39, No. 2 (April): 237-261.

FAO. 2003. "Honduras" in *WTO Agreement on Agriculture: The Implementation Experience – Developing Country Case Studies*. Accessed January 2012. http://www.fao.org/DOCREP/005/Y4632E/Y4632E00.HTM

_____ 2009. "From Land Grab to Win-Win: Seizing the Opportunities of International Investments in Agriculture" FAO Policy Brief, June. Accessed February 2012. Available at: http://www.fao.org/economic/es-policybriefs/briefs-detail/en/?no_cache=1&uid=21523

_____ 2011. "Price Monitoring and Analysis Country Brief: Honduras, January-April 2011." Accessed May 2012. http://www.fao.org/docrep/014/am581e/am581e00.pdf

_____ 2012. "Perfiles sobre la pesca y la acuicultura por países: Honduras"

FAO Fisheries and Aquaculture Department. Accessed July 2012. http://www.fao.org/fishery/countrysector/FI-CP_HN/es

FIAN. 2012. "International Organisations condemn repression and criminalisation of peasant organisations of the Bajo Aguán, Honduras" FIAN International, Aug. 30, 2012. Accessed October 2012. http://www.fian.org/news/news/international-organisations-condemn-repression-and-criminalisation-of-peasant-organisations-of-the-bajo-aguan-honduras

_____ 2000. "The Right to Adequate Food in Honduras" Initial Report (Art. 1-15) of Honduras to the Committee on Economic, Social and Cultural Rights. UN Doc E/1990/5/Add.40.

FIAN et al. 2011. "Honduras: Human Rights Violations in Bajo Aguán" International Fact Finding Mission Report, July 2011. Accessed August 2011. http://www.fian.org/resources/documents/others/honduras-human-rights-violations-in-bajo-aguan/pdf

FIDH. 2011. "Honduras: Human Rights Violations in Bajo Aguán" Federación Internacional de Derechos Humanos, Report No. 572a. September 2011. Accessed April 2012. http://www.fidh.org/IMG/pdf/honduras573ang.pdf

Foroohar, Manzar. 2011. "Palestinians in Central America: From temporary emigrants to a permanent diaspora" *Journal of Palestine Studies*, 11, No. 3 (Spring): 6-22.

FOSDEH, COCOCH and ILC. n.d. "Antecedentes Históricos de la Reforma Agraria en Honduras." International Land Coalition. Accessed April 2012. http://americalatina.landcoalition.org/node/1746

Frank, Dana. 2010. "Out of the Past, a New Honduran Culture of Resistance" *NACLA Report on the Americas,* May/June. Accessed October 2012. https://nacla.org/article/out-past-new-honduran-culture-resistance

_____ 2011. "WikiLeaks Honduras: US Linked to Brutal Businessman" *The Nation.* October 21, 2011. Accessed January 2012. http://www.thenation.com/article/164120/wikileaks-honduras-us-linked-brutal-businessman

_____ 2012. "Honduras: Which Side is the US On?" *The Nation.* May 22, 2012. Accessed August 2012. http://www.thenation.com/article/167994/honduras-which-side-us

FTF (Feed the Future). 2010. "Honduras: FY 2010 Implementation Plan" US government working document. Accessed January 2012. Available at: http://www.feedthefuture.gov/country/honduras

_____ 2011. "Honduras: FY2011-2015 Multi-Year Strategy" US government document. Accessed Feb. 2012. Available at: http://www.feedthefuture.gov/country/honduras

GAIA. n.d. "What is the Clean Development Mechanism?" Global Alliance for Incinerator Alternatives (GAIA) Fact Sheet. Accessed May 2012. http://no-burn.org/downloads/GAIA_CDMFactsheet.pdf

Glodhaber-Fiebert et al. 2011. "Multi-Country analysis of palm oil consumption and cardiovascular disease mortality for countries at different stages of economic development: 1980-1997" *Globalization and Health* 7, No. 45.

González, Nancie L. 1992. *Dollar, Dove and Eagle: One hundred years of*

Palestinian migration to Honduras. Ann Arbor: University of Michigan Press.

Gould, B. 1986. *Empresas Campesinas en Honduras: El Modelo y la Realidad.* Inter-American Institute for Cooperation on Agriculture, Fortalecimiento de la Capacidad Gerencial de Empresas Campesinas de Producción Agropecuaria.

GRAIN. 2007. "Corporate Power: The Palm Oil – Biodiesel Nexus" *Seedling*, July. Accessed April 2012. http://www.grain.org/article/entries/611-corporate-power-the-palm-oil-biodiesel-nexus

_____ 2008. *Seized! The 2008 Land Grab for Food and Financial Security.* GRAIN Briefing, October. Accessed July 2012. http://www.grain.org/article/entries/93-seized-the-2008-landgrab-for-food-and-financial-security

_____ 2010. "Land grabs threaten Anuak" April 13, 2010. Accessed July 2011. http://www.grain.org/article/entries/4064-land-grabs-threaten-anuak

_____ 2011a. "Pension Funds: Key players in the global farmland grab" June 29, 2011. Accessed July 2012. http://farmlandgrab.org/post/view/18864

_____ 2011b. "Land Grabbing and the Global Food Crisis" Slideshare presentation. December 2011. Accessed July 2012. Available from: http://www.grain.org/article/entries/4164-land-grabbing-and-the-global-food-crisis-presentation

_____ 2012. "GRAIN releases data set with over 400 global land grabs" February 23, 2012. Accessed July 2012. http://www.grain.org/article/entries/4479-grain-releases-data-set-with-over-400-global-land-grabs

Greenpeace. 2007. "How the Oil Palm Industry is Cooking the Climate" Nov. 8, 2007. Accessed March 2012. http://www.greenpeace.org.uk/media/reports/cooking-the-climate

Guity, Ericka. 2009. "A Case of Violation of the Right to Food: Community of Triunfo de la Cruz" *Red Sugar, Green Desserts.* FIAN International, December. Accessed June 2012. http://independent.academia.edu/ErickaGuity/Papers/1203052/A_case_of_violation_of_the_right_to_food_community_of_Triunfo_de_la_Cruz_Honduras

Hai Teoh, Cheng. 2011. "Key Sustainability Issues in the Palm Oil Sector: A Discussion Paper for Multi-Stakeholders Consultations." Commissioned by the World Bank Group International Finance Corporation. Accessed April 2012. http://www.ifc.org/ifcext/agriconsultation.nsf/Attachments ByTitle/Discussion+Paper/$FILE/Discussion+Paper_FINAL.pdf

Harborne, Alaistar R., Daniel C. Azfal and Mark J. Andrews. 2001. "Honduras: Caribbean Coast" *Marine Pollution Bulletin* 42, No. 12: 1221-1235.

Hari, Johann. 2010. "The Wrong Kind of Green" *The Nation*, March 22, 2010. Accessed July 2012. http://www.thenation.com/article/wrong-kind-green#

Harvey, David. 2005. *A Brief History of Neoliberalism.* Oxford University Press.

Haupt, D.E., G. Drinkard and H.F. Pierce. 1984. "Future of Petrochemical Raw Materials in Oleochemical Markets" *Journal of Petrochemical Raw Materials* 61, No. 2 (February).

Hawkes, Corina. 2006. "Uneven dietary development: linking the policies and processes of globalization with the nutrition transition, obesity and diet-related chronic diseases" *Globalization and Health* 2, No. 4.

Herndon, Andrew. 2012. "SG Biofuels Gets $17 Million to Develop Bioenergy Crop Jatropha" Bloomberg, January 17, 2012. Accessed April 2012. http://www.bloomberg.com/news/2012-01-17/sg-biofuels-gets-17-million-to-develop-bioenergy-crop-jatropha.html

Hodge, James and Melissa Cooper. 2009. "U.S. continues to train Honduran soldiers" *Presente!* July 2009. Accessed August 2012. http://www.soaw.org/presente/index.php?option=com_content&task=view&id=225&Itemid=74

Holt-Giménez, Eric. 2007. "LAND – GOLD – REFORM: The Territorial Restructuring of Guatemala's Highlands" Food First Development Report No. 16, September. Accessed April 2012. Available at: http://www.foodfirst.org/en/node/1770

———— 2010. "Linking Farmers' Movements for Advocacy and Practice" *The Journal of Peasant Studies* 37, No. 1 (January): 203–236.

Honduras Culture and Politics. "Minimum Wage or Living Wage?" Sept. 6, 2010. Accessed July 2012. http://hondurasculturepolitics.blogspot.com/2010/09/minimum-wage-or-living-wage.html

———— 2011. "New U.S. Bases in Honduras" November 28, 2011. Accessed July 2012. http://hondurasculturepolitics.blogspot.com/2011/11/new-us-bases-in-honduras.html

Howard-Borjas, Patricia. 1995. "Cattle and crisis: The genesis of unsustainable development in Central America" *Land Reform, Land Settlement and Cooperatives*, 88-116. Accessed April 2012. Available at: http://www.fao.org/docrep/V9828T/v9828t10.htm

IACHR. 2012. "IACHR Condemns Murder of Human Rights Defenders in Honduras" Press Release, Sept. 28 2012. Accessed October 2012. http://www.oas.org/en/iachr/media_center/PReleases/2012/121.asp

———— 2010-2011. "Indigenous and Tribal Peoples' Rights Over Their Ancestral Lands and Natural Resources: Norms and Jurisprudence of the Inter-American Human Rights System" *American Indian Law Review* 35, No. 2: 263-496.

IIC. 2009. "IIC approves loan to Grupo DINANT Companies in Honduras" June 16, 2009. Accessed February 2012. http://finpyme.iic.org/media/press/2011-11-23/iic-approves-loan-grupo-dinant-companies-honduras

IICA. 2010. "Atlas de la agroenergía y los biocombustibles en las Américas" Instituto Interamericano de Cooperación para la Agricultura (IICA), Programa Hemisférico en Agroenergía y Biocombustibles. San José, C.R.

IDB. 2005. "IDB approves $35 million loan to Honduras for sustainable tourism program" Accessed July 2012. http://www.iadb.org/en/news/news-releases/2005-05-04/idb-approves-35-million-loan-to-honduras-for-sustainable-tourism-program,1833.html

IFC. 1997. "IFC to Finance Honduran Manufacturing and Agribusiness Company" International Finance Corporation (press release) June 26, 1997. Accessed February 2012. www.ifc.org/ifcext/mediahub.nsf/Content/SelectedPR?OpenDocument&UNID=CF9FB05A80C52CBA85256977004B4B44

———— 2009a. "Corporacion Dinant S.A. de C.V." IFC Summary of

Proposed Investment. Accessed February 2012. http://www.ifc.org/
ifcext/spiwebsite1.nsf/0/2F9B9D3AFCF1F894852576BA000E2CD0

_____ 2009b. "Oleoproductos de Honduras S.A. de C.V." IFC Summary
of Proposed Investment. Accessed February 2012. http://www.ifc.org/
ifcext/spiwebsite1.nsf/0/E90F482EEA0BE2C9852576BA000E2D34

_____ 2011. "The World Bank Group Framework and IFC
Strategy for Engagement in the Palm Oil Sector" March 21, 2011.
Accessed February 2012. www.ifc.org/ifcext/agriconsultation.nsf/
AttachmentsByTitle/Final_PO+paper_Mar2011/$FILE/WBG+
Framework+and+IFC+Strategy_FINAL_FOR+WEB.pdf

Jakarta Post, The. 2012. "Chinese tycoons join politics for survival" Jan.
14, 2012. Accessed February 2012. http://www.thejakartapost.com/
news/2012/01/24/chinese-tycoons-join-politics-survival.html

Janson, Kees and Esther Roquas. 1998. "Modernizing Insecurity: The Land
Titling Project in Honduras" *Development and Change* 29: 81-106.

Jeffrey, Paul. 1998. "After the Storm" *The Christian Century*. November 18,
1998.

_____ 1999. "Rhetoric and Reconstruction in Post-Mitch Honduras"
NACLA Report on the Americas, Vol. XXXIII, No. 2 (September/October).

_____ 2002. "Looking to Ourselves: The Response to Hurricane Mitch
in the Lower Aguán Valley" *Deciphering Honduras: Four Views of Post-Mitch
Political Reality*, eds. Torres Calderón et al. Cambridge, MA: Hemisphere
Initiatives.

Jones, Jeffrey R. 1990. *Colonization and Environment: Land Settlement Projects
in Central America.* The United Nations University.

Juventud Rebelde. 2009. "Starvation predicted in Honduras" Dec. 29, 2009.
Accessed Jan. 2012. http://hondurasoye.wordpress.com/2009/12/31/
starvation-predicted-in-honduras/

Kay, Cristóbal. 2008. "Reflections on Latin American Rural Studies in the
Neoliberal Globalization Period: A New Rurality?" *Development and
Change* 39, No. 6: 915-943.

Kiple, Kennet F. and Kriemhield Cornee Ornelas, eds. 2000. "Palm Oil" in
Cambridge World History of Food. Cambridge University Press.

Klein, Naomi. 2005. "The Rise of Disaster Capitalism" *The Nation*, April
14, 2005.

_____ 2007. *The Shock Doctrine.* New York: Metropolitan Books.

Kongsager, R. and A. Reenberg. 2012. "Contemporary Land-Use Transitions:
The global oil palm expansion" GLP Report No. 4. Copenhagen:
GLP-IPO.

LaFeber, Walter. 1984. *Inevitable Revolutions: The United States in Central
America.* New York: W.W. Norton.

La Prensa. 2008a. "Decreto ahuyenta las inversiones" May 28, 2008. Reprinted
by CentralAmericaData. Accessed May 2012. http://en.centralamericadata.
com/es/article/home/Honduras_Decreto_ahuyenta_las_inversiones

_____ 2008b. "Militares salen a las calles a vender frijoles" July 26, 2008.
Accessed July 2012. http://archivo.laprensa.hn/content/view/full/2266

_____ 2008c. "Bajos precios de la palma provocan crisis" December 2,

2008 Accessed April 2012. http://archivo.laprensa.hn/Negocios/Ediciones /2008/12/03/Noticias/Bajos-precios-de-la-palma-provocan-crisis

_____ 2009. "Palmeros generarán 2,600 galones de biodiesel" March 12, 2009. Accessed April 2012. http://archivo.laprensa.hn/ Negocios/Ediciones/2009/03/13/Noticias/Palmeros-generaran-2-600-galones-de-biodiesel

_____ 2011. "Aprobada ley que da vida a ciudad modelo" July 28, 2011. Accessed March 2012. http://archivo.laprensa.hn/Ediciones/2011/07/ 29/Noticias/Aprobada-ley-que-da-vida-a-ciudad-modelo

La Tribuna. 2008. "A reunión de emergencia el COHEP para impugnar decreto" December 28, 2008. Accessed July 2012. http://old.latribuna. hn/2008/12/28/post10052479/

_____ 2011. "Avanza Centro de Conservación de Vida Silvestre y la orga-nización de jóvenes comunicadores" January 15, 2012. Accessed August 2012. http://www.latribuna.hn/2012/01/15/avanza-centro-de-conser-vacion-de-vida-silvestre-y-la-organizacion-de-jovenes-comunicadores/

_____ 2012a. "Maquiladores piden acelerar proyecto de ciudades modelo" March 12, 2012. Accessed July 2012. http://www.latribuna.hn/2012/03/ 12/maquiladores-piden-acelerar-proyecto-de-ciudades-modelo/

_____ 2012b. "Lobo y MUCA suscriben acuerdo para pago de tierras en el Aguán" June 6, 2012. Accessed June 2012. http://www.latribuna. hn/2012/06/06/lobo-y-muca-suscriben-acuerdo-para-pago-de-tierras-en-el-aguan/

La Voz de Zácate Grande. 2012. "Comunicado: Movimiento de Recuperación y titulación de las Tierras y Liberación de las playas de Zácate Grande." January 19, 2012. Accessed August 2012. http://zacategrande.blogspot. com/2012/01/comunicado-facusse-traves-de-los-medios.html

LeFevre, Anne Germain and Miguel Humberto Ramírez. 2010. "Primera Aproximación a las Oportunidades y Amenazas de los Biocombustibles en Centroamérica" San Salvador: FUNDE, February 2010.

LIBRE. 2012. "Declaración de Principios de Libertad y Refundación" February 20, 2012. Accessed June 2012. http://libertadyrefundacion. com/?q=node/17

Lindsay-Poland, John. 2011. "Honduras and the U.S. Military" Fellowship of Reconciliation (FOR), September 21, 2011. Accessed September 2011. http://forusa.org/blogs/john-lindsay-poland/honduras-us-military/ 9943#11

_____ 2012. "Honduras Grows as Pentagon Hub in Central America" FOR, March 1, 2012. Accessed March 2012. http://forusa.org/blogs/ john-lindsay-poland/honduras-grows-pentagon-hub-central-america/ 10311

Lipton, Eric. 2010. "Private Links in Lawmaker's Trip Abroad" *New York Times*, December 19, 2010. Accessed April 2012. http:// www.nytimes.com/2010/12/20/world/americas/20inquire.html ?pagewanted=1&_r=2&sq=rohrabacher&st=cse&scp=1

Macías, Miguel Alonzo. 2001. *La Capital de la Contrarreforma Agraria: el Bajo-Aguán de Honduras.* Tegucigalpa: Editorial Guaymuras

Mahoney, James. 2001. *The Legacies of Liberalism: Path Dependence and Political Regimes in Central America*. Baltimore, MA: John Hopkins University Press.

Marcouiller, David and Raymond Robertson. 2009. "Globalization and Working Conditions: Evidence from Honduras" *Globalization, Wages, and the Quality of Jobs: Five Country Studies*, eds. Robertson et al. Washington, DC: World Bank.

Marquardt, Steve. 2001. "Green Havoc: Panama Disease, Environmental Change, and Labor Process in the Central American Banana Industry" *The American Historical Review*, Vol. 106, No. 1.

May I Speak Freely? 2008. "The Rev. James Francis Guadalupe Carney" Last Updated September 9, 2008. Accessed May 2012. http://mayispeakfreely.org/index.php?gSec=doc&doc_id=17

McCain, Greg. 2012. "The DEA and the Return of Deathsquads" Counterpunch. June 15-17, 2012. Accessed July 2012. http://www.counterpunch.org/2012/06/15/the-dea-and-the-return-of-the-death-squads/

McMichael, Philip. 2004. "Global development and the corporate food regime" Paper read at Symposium on New Directions in the Sociology of Global Development, XI World Congress of Rural Sociology.

_____ 2009. "A Food Regime Genealogy" *The Journal of Peasant Studies* 36, No. 1 (January): 139-169.

_____ 2012. "The Land Grab and Corporate Food Regime Restructuring" *The Journal of Peasant Studies* 39, No. 3-4 (July-October): 681-701.

Mejía, Thelma. 2009. "Economy-Honduras: Stormy Outlook for 2009" Inter-Press News Service (IPS) January 6, 2009. Accessed July 2012. http://www.ipsnews.net/2009/01/economy-honduras-stormy-outlook-for-2009/

_____ 2011. "Honduras: Dying for Land" Inter-Press News Service (IPS) Sept. 5, 2011. Accessed July 2012. http://www.ipsnews.net/2011/09/honduras-dying-for-land/

Méndez, Luis. 2009. "Relación de familias que financiaron el Golpe en Honduras" *Aporrea*, August 16, 2009. Accessed April 2012. http://www.aporrea.org/internacionales/a84643.html

Meritas, 2010. *Guía Legal de Negocios Para América Latina y el Caribe*. Minneapolis, MN: Meritas, Inc.

Merrill, Tim. 1995. *Honduras: A Country Study*. Washington: GPO for the Library of Congress. Accessed September 2011. http://countrystudies.us/honduras/20.htm

Meyer, Peter J. 2011. "Honduran-U.S. Relations" CRS Report for Congress, July 14, 2011.

_____ 2012. "Honduran-U.S. Relations" CRS Report for Congress, April 25, 2012.

MUCA. 2010a. *MUCA: Machete de Esperanza*. Accessed May 2012. Available at: http://www.scribd.com/doc/45288788/Movimiento-Campesino-del-Aguan-MUCA-Honduras

MUCA. 2010b. "Recuento de los Hechos y la Recuperación de las Tierras de la Reforma Agraria en Honduras" Movimiento Campesino del Aguán (MUCA). Article republished by Alba TV, January 13, 2010. Accessed

May 2012. http://albatv.org/Recuento-de-los-hechos-y-la.html

NCDC. 2009. "Mitch: The Deadliest Atlantic Hurricane Since 1780" US Department of Commerce National Climatic Data Center. Last updated January 23, 2009. Accessed August 2012. http://lwf.ncdc.noaa.gov/oa/reports/mitch/mitch.html

Nelson, Richard T. 2003. "Honduras Country Brief: Property Rights and Land Markets" Madison, WI: University of Wisconsin Land Tenure Center, June.

New Internationalist. 1982. "Battling For A Bigger Slice Of Banana" *New Internationalist*, No. 108 (February). Accessed October 2012. http://www.newint.org/features/1982/02/01/banana/

Nuila Coto, Ramón Wilberto. 2010. "Palma Africana Ecológica: Honduras compite con grandes productores mundiales responsables con el medio ambiente" Corporación Dinant, June 16, 2010. Accessed July 2012. http://www.dinant.com/noticias.php?noti_id=86&start=0&categoria_id=&prede_id=&arcyear=&arcmonth=

OFRANEH. 2010a. "213 años de resistencia del pueblo garífuna" Vos el Soberano, March 11, 2010. Accessed July 2012. http://voselsoberano.com/v1/index.php?option=com_content&view=article&id=4560:213-anos-de-resistencia-del-pueblo-garifuna&catid=1:noticias-generales

_____ 2010b. "El artículo del Rey del Porno en el Heraldo (del golpismo)" BellaCiao, August 6, 2010. Accessed March 2012. http://bellaciao.org/es/spip.php?article7299

_____ 2012. "El Banana Coast y la expulsión de los garífunas de la bahía de Trujillo" Accessed July 2012. http://www.youtube.com/watch?feature=player_embedded&v=6PhVwV-RvCc

Olanchito Noticias. 2012. "Campesinos reclaman tierras a la Standard Fruit de Honduras" January 12, 2012. Accessed May 2012. http://www.youtube.com/watch?v=Bbb3bDspb7U

Oxfam. 2008. "A Life with Dignity: Honduran women raising voices to improve labour standards" Speaking Out Programme Insights. Oxfam GB, November.

_____ 2011. *Land and Power: The growing scandal surrounding the new wave of investments in land*. Oxfam Briefing Paper, September 22, 2011.

Paley, Dawn. 2010. "The Honduran Business Elite One Year After the Coup" NACLA, June 23, 2010. Accessed July 2012. https://nacla.org/node/6619

_____ 2012. "Charter Cities in Honduras: A proposal to expand Canadian colonialism" *Upside Down World*, April 26, 2012. Accessed May 2012. http://upsidedownworld.org/main/news-briefs-archives-68/3600-charter-cities-in-honduras-a-proposal-to-expand-canadian-colonialism

PalmOil HQ. 2009. "How palm oil helps feed an increasingly hungry world" November 16, 2009. Accessed May 2012. http://www.palmoilhq.com/PalmOilNews/how-palm-oil-helps-feed-an-increasingly-hungry-world/

Panapanaan, Virgilio et al. 2009. "Sustainability of Palm Oil Production and Opportunities for Finnish Technology and Know-How

Transfer" Lappeenranta University of Technology, Institute of Energy Technology Research Report 1, March. Accessed April 2012. Available at: http://www.scribd.com/doc/87048860/31/Recent-and-on-going-CDM-projects-on-palm-oil

Payne Roberts, Caitlin. 2011. "Voices of Non-violent Resistance: Rural Community Radio in Honduras" Food First, July 21, 2011. Accessed July 2012. http://www.foodfirst.org/en/node/3519

Paz, Will. 2011. "Denuncia MUCA-Margen Izquierda: Rechazamos Campaña Defamatoria" Honduras Contra el Golpe de Estado, August 17, 2011. Accessed June 2012. http://hondurascontraelgolpedeestado.blogspot.com/2011/08/denuncia-muca-margen.html

Pehnelt, Gernot and Christoph Vietze. 2010. "European Policies towards Palm Oil—Sorting Out Some Facts" GlobEcon Research Paper 01. Accessed April 2012. http://www.globecon.org/fileadmin/template/userfiles/Research/PalmOilGlobEcon.pdf

Pollan, Michael. 2008. In Defense of Food: An Eater's Manifesto. New York: Penguin Press.

Popkin, B. 1999. "Urbanization, lifestyle changes and the nutrition transition" World Development 27, No. 11: 1905–1916.

Prensa Latina. 2011. "Can Honduras Be a Part of Petrocaribe Again?" Translated and reprinted by Emerging Terrains News. December 25, 2011. Accessed March 2012. http://emergingterrains.com/investmentnews/honduras/can-honduras-be-a-part-of-petrocaribe-again/

Prieto-Carrón, Marina, Marilyn Thomson and Mandy Macdonald. 2007. "No more killings! Women respond to femicides in Central America" Gender & Development 15, No. 1.

Proceso Digital. 2011. "En noviembre de 2010, CSJ declaró inconstitucional decreto de expropiación forzosa de tierras en Honduras" January 18, 2011. Accessed May 2012. http://www.proceso.hn/2011/01/18/Nacionales/En.noviembre.de/32627.html

Real News, The. 2010. "Honduran campesinos under the gun Part 2" April 20, 2010. Accessed June 2012. http://www.youtube.com/watch?v=Gyh3FbbjQMk

Regalado, María Luisa. 2011. "CODEMUH: Women's Resistance in Honduras" Upside Down World, March 22, 2011. Accessed July 2012. http://upsidedownworld.org/main/honduras-archives-46/2963-codemuh-womens-resistance-in-honduras

Reuters. 2008. "RPT-FACTBOX-The world's top 15 listed palm oil companies" March 11, 2008. Accessed July 2012. http://in.reuters.com/article/2008/03/11/malaysia-palm-idINKLR12924920080311

Richardson, D.L. 1995. "The History of Oil Palm Breeding in the United Fruit Company" ASD Oil Palm Papers No. 11. Accessed June 2012. http://www.asd-cr.com/paginas/english/articulos/bol11-1en.html

Richardson, Jill. 2011. "Worst Food Additive Ever?" Alternet. Oct. 24, 2011. Accessed February 2012. http://www.alternet.org/story/152848/worst_food_additive_ever_it's_in_half_of_all_foods_we_eat_and_its_production_destroys_rainforests_and_enslaves_children?page=entire

Ríos, Gilberto. 2010. "Reforma Agraria y el Conflicto Agrario en el Bajo Aguán" FIAN International – Sección Honduras. February 2, 2010.

_____ 2010b. "Violencia y muerte en el Valle del Aguán: Antecedentes del conflicto por la Tierra" Vos el Soberano. November 15, 2010. Accessed June 2012. http://voselsoberano.com/v1/index.php?option=com_cont ent&view=article&id=8326:violencia-y-muerte-en-el-valle-del-aguan-antecedentes-del-conflicto-por-la-tierra&catid=1:noticias-generales

Rocha, José Luis. 2010. "Remittances in Central America: Whose money is it anyway?" *American Sociological Association* 17, No. 2.

Rodríguez, James. 2008. "Honduras: Garifuna Resistance to Mega-Tourism in Tela Bay" Upside Down World, August 6, 2008. Accessed July 2012. http://upsidedownworld.org/main/honduras-archives-46/1409-honduras-garifuna-resistance-to-mega-tourism-in-tela-bay

_____ 2010. "La Historia se Repite: Comité de Familiares de Detenidos-Desaparecidos de Honduras" MiMundo. February 7, 2010. Accessed August 2012. http://www.mimundo-fotorreportajes.org/2010/02/la-historia-se-repite-comite-de.html

Romer, Paul and Brandon Fuller. 2011. "Special Development Regions in Honduras" Charter Cities. Accessed February 2012. www.chartercities. org/file_download/18/Honduras+Update+Dec+2011.pdf

Romer, Paul and Octavio Sánchez. 2012. "Urban Prosperity in the RED" *The Globe and Mail*. April 25, 2012. Accessed April 2012. http://www.theglo-beandmail.com/news/opinions/opinion/urban-prosperity-in-the-red/article2412947/

Rosset, Peter. 2011. "Food Sovereignty and Alternative Paradigms to Confront Land Grabbing and the Food and Climate Crises" *Development* 54, No. 1: 21–30.

Rosset, Peter, Raj Patel and Michael Courville, eds. 2006. *Promised Land: Competing Visions of Agrarian Reform.* Oakland: Food First Books.

Ruhl, Mark. 1984. "Agrarian Structure and Political Stability in Honduras" *Journal of Interamerican Studies and World Affairs* 26, No. 1 (February): 33-68.

Rulli, Javiera. 2009. "WWF siervo del Agronegocio y de la glo-balización" EcoPortal, September 12, 2009. Accessed July 2012. http://www.ecoportal.net/Temas_Especiales/Globalizacion/wwf_siervo_del_agronegocio_y_de_la_globalizacion

Rupilius, Wolfgang and Salmia Ahmad. 2005. "The Changing World of Oleochemicals" *Palm Oil Developments* 44: 15-28.

Ryan, Ramor. 2008. "The Last Rebels of the Caribbean: Garifuna Fighting for Their Lives in Honduras" *Upside Down World*. March 27, 2008. Accessed March 2012. http://upsidedownworld.org/main/content/view/1195/1/

SAG. 2009. "Cadena de Cultivos Bioenergéticos" Secretaria de Agricultura y Ganadería (SAG). Accessed March 2012. http://www.sag.gob.hn/files/Agronegocios/Oportunidades/cultivos_bio.pdf

Sanders, Arie, Angélica Ramírez y Lilian Morazán. 2006. *Cadenas Agrícolas en Honduras: Desarrollo Socioeconómico y Ambiente.* Valle de Yeguare, Honduras: Escuela Agrícola Panamericana, Zamorano. Document presented to IFPRI, December 2006.

Shanker, Thom. 2012. "Lessons of Iraq Help U.S. Fight a Drug War in Honduras" New York Times, May 5, 2012. Accessed July 2012. http://www.nytimes.com/2012/05/06/world/americas/us-turns-its-focus-on-drug-smuggling-in-honduras.html?pagewanted=all

Sharma, Dinesh C. 2012. "Indian diet proves to be an increasingly oily affair" Daily Mail Online India, April 1, 2012. Accessed April 2012. http://www.dailymail.co.uk/indiahome/indianews/article-2123600/Indian-diet-proves-increasingly-oily-affair.html#ixzz1soskjc2x

Shattuck, Annie. 2009. "Will Sustainability Certifications Work? A look at the Roundtable on Sustainable Biofuels" *Agrofuels in the Americas*. Oakland: Food First Books, 118-132.

SICE. 2012. "EU and Central America sign Association Agreement (Press Release)" Organization of American State's Foreign Trade Information System (SICE), June 29, 2012. Accessed August 2012. Available at: http://www.sice.oas.org/

Spring, Karen. 2011. "Canadian Porn Kings, Tourism 'Development' Projects, Repression & the Violation of Indigenous Garifuna Rights in Honduras" Rights Action. February 14, 2011. Accessed March 2012. http://rightsaction.org/articles/Garifuna_repression_021711.html

Stonich, Susan. 2008. "International Tourism and Disaster Capitalism: The Case of Hurricane Mitch in Honduras" *Capitalizing On Catastrophe: Neoliberal Strategies in Disaster Reconstruction*, eds. Nandini Gunewardena and Mark Schuller. Lanham, MD: Altamira Press, 47-68.

Sun Daily, The (Malaysia). 2012. "Palm-biofuels fail to meet US green standards: EPA" January 29, 2012. Accessed April 2012. http://www.thesundaily.my/news/279082

Terra. 2011. "Walmart inunda con tiendas el mercado de consumo" December 29, 2011. Accessed Jan. 2012. http://economia.terra.com.co/noticias/noticia.aspx?idNoticia=201112292318INF80663402

Thoenes, P. 2006. "Biofuels and Commodity Markets – Palm Oil Focus" Paper based on a presentation made at AgraInforma conference *The Impact of biofuels on commodity markets*, Brussels, October 24-25, 2006. Accessed May 2012. http://faorlc.cgnet.com/es/prioridades/bioenergia/pdf/commodity.pdf

Thorpe, Andy. 2002. *Agrarian Modernisation in Honduras*. Latin American Studies Series, Vol. 18. Lewiston, NY: The Edwin Mellen Press.

Torres Calderón, Manuel. 2002. "Who Knows Honduras?" in *Deciphering Honduras: Four Views of Post-Mitch Political Reality*, eds. Torres Calderón et al. Cambridge, MA: Hemisphere Initiatives.

Trucchi, Giorgio. 2008. "The Pellas Group and Agrofuels: They Want to Plant Sugarcane in the Most Productive Food Producing Area" *Rel-UITA*. March 27, 2008. Accessed March 2012. http://www.rel-uita.org/agricultura/agrocombustibles/el_grupo_pellas_eng.htm

_____ 2010. "De Nuevo Corre Sangre en el Bajo Aguán" *AlbaSud*, November 23, 2010. Accessed June 2012. http://www.albasud.org/noticia/es/135/de-nuevo-corre-la-sangre-en-el-bajo-aguan

_____ 2011. "Interview with Juan Ramón Chinchilla, MUCA" *Honduras:*

Human Rights, January 14, 2011. Accessed October 2012. http://hondurashumanrights.wordpress.com/2011/01/14/interview-with-juan-ramon-chinchilla-muca/

_____ 2012. "They want to strangle us financially" *Rel-UITA*, January 24, 2012. Accessed June 2012. http://www.rel-uita.org/agricultura/palma_africana/quieren_asfixiarnos_economicamente-eng.htm

Trucchi, Giorgio and Lorena Zelaya. 2010. "Boicot a los productos de Miguel Facussé (Corporación Dinant)" *Lista Informativa Nicaragua y Más*, December 9, 2010. Accessed May 2012. http://nicaraguaymasespanol.blogspot.com/2010/12/boicot-los-productos-de-miguel-facusse.html

UNEP. 2011. "Oil palm plantations: threats and opportunities for tropical ecosystems" UNEP Global Environmental Alert Service (GEAS). Accessed April 2012. http://www.unep.org/pdf/Dec_11_Palm_Plantations.pdf

UNESCO. 2012. "Director-General condemns killing of Honduran journalist José Noel Canales Lagos and calls for end to impunity for such murders" UNESCOPRESS, August 19, 2012. Accessed August 2012. http://www.unesco.org/new/en/media-services/single-view/news/director_general_condemns_killing_of_honduran_journalist_jose_noel_canales_lagos_and_calls_for_end_to_impunity_for_such_murders/

Unilever. 2000. "Unilever to acquire Grupo Cressida" (Press Release) February 3, 2000. Accessed February 2012. https://www.unilever.com/mediacentre/pressreleases/2000/grupo.aspx

USAID. 2011a. "USAID and Walmart Join Forces to Help Small Farmers and Enhance Food Security in Central America" (Press Release) March 11, 2011. Accessed Jan. 2012. http://www.usaid.gov/press/releases/2011/pr110322_1.html

USAID. 2011b. "Country Profile: Property Rights and Resource Governance Honduras" April 2011. Accessed July 2012. http://www.usaidlandtenure.net/country-profiles/honduras

US Commercial Service. 2011. "Doing Business in Honduras: 2011 Country Commercial Guide for U.S. Companies." US & Foreign Commercial Service and US Department of State, 2011. Accessed March 2012. http://www.buyusainfo.net/docs/x_8235548.pdf

US Embassy. 2004. "Honduras: Fast-Food Boom Continues as First Quiznos Opens" US Embassy in Tegucigalpa. Created Oct. 5, 2004. Cable released by WikiLeaks Aug. 30, 2011. Accessed April 2012. http://dazzlepod.com/cable/04TEGUCIGALPA2223/

USDA-FAS. 2010. "Biofuels Annual" USDA Foreign Agriculture Service Global Agricultural Information Network (GAIN) Report No. HO1005. July 13, 2010.

_____ 2012a. "Honduras Exporter Guide" USDA Foreign Agriculture Service Global Agricultural Information Network (GAIN) Report. January 27, 2012.

_____ 2012b. "Honduras Biofuels Annual" USDA Foreign Agriculture Service Global Agricultural Information Network (GAIN) Report, July 3, 2012.

USTR. 2009. "Honduras" United States Trade Representative (USTR) Report. Accessed April 2012. http://www.ustr.gov/sites/default/files/uploads/reports/2010/NTE/2010_NTE_Honduras_final.pdf

Vamos al Grano. 2012. "Conflicto agrario en el Bajo Aguán: el caso MUCA" March 3, 2012. Accessed June 2012. http://www.vamosal-grano.org/publicaciones/item/conflicto-agrario-en-el-bajo-aguan-el-caso-muca?category_id=6

Vía Campesina. 2007. "Declaration of Nyéléni" Food Sovereignty Forum, Nyéléni Village, Selingue, Mali. February 27, 2007. Accessed June 2012. http://viacampesina.org/en/index.php?option=com_content&task=view&id=282&Itemid

Vía Campesina et al. 2011. "Ley de Transformación Agraria Integral" October 11, 2011. Accessed June 2012. http://www.vamosalgrano.org/images/generales/descargas/generales/leyagraria.pdf

Vos el Soberno. 2009. "Diez familias financiaron el Golpe de Estado en Honduras" August 1, 2009. Accessed March 2012. http://voselsoberano.com/v1/index.php?option=com_content&view=article&id=78%3Adiez-familias-financiaron-el-golpe-de-estado-en-honduras-vea-lista-de-empresas&catid=10%3Aautores-del-golpe&Itemid=5

———— 2011. "Quienes Quebraron CONADI? Raíces históricas de la fortuna de Miguel Facussé Barjum" June 11, 2011. Accessed July 2012. http://voselsoberano.com/v1/index.php?option=com_content&view=article&id=11667%3Aiquienes-quebraron-conadi-raices-historicas-de-la-fortuna-de-miguel-facusse-barjum&catid=1%3Anoticias-generales&Itemid=8

Wahid, Mohd Basri, W.S. Lim and S. Arif. 2007. "Technological Development and New Growth Areas of the Oil Palm Industry" *Oil Palm Industry Economic Journal* 7, No. 1.

Wise, Timothy A. 2009. "Promise or pitfall? The limited gains from agricultural trade liberalization for developing countries" *Journal of Peasant Studies* 36, No. 4, 855-870

White, Ben, Saturnino M. Borras Jr., Ruth Hall, Ian Scoones and Wendy Wolford. 2012. "The New Enclosures: Critical perspectives on corporate land deals" *The Journal of Peasant Studies* 39, No. 3-4 (July-October): 619-647.

World Bank. 1995. "Program Completion Report. Republic of Honduras Structural Adjustment Loan II and Structural Adjustment Credit" Report No. 13884. January 20, 1995.

———— 2010. "Rising Global Interest in Farmland: Can it yield sustainable and equitable benefits?" Washington, DC: World Bank.

———— 2011. "The World Bank Group Framework and IFC Strategy for Engagement in the Palm Oil Sector" International Finance Corporation. Accessed Jan. 2012. http://www.ifc.org/ifcext/agriconsultation.nsf/Content/keydocuments

World Growth. 2011. "The Economic Benefit of Palm Oil to Indonesia" World Growth Palm Oil Green Development Campaign, February 2011. Accessed May 2012. http://www.worldgrowth.org/assets/files/

WG_Indonesian_Palm_Oil_Benefits_Report-2_11.pdf

World Rainforest Movement. 2006. "Oil Palm: from Cosmetics to Biodiesel, Colonization Lives On." September 2006. Accessed July 2012. Available at: http://www.wrm.org.uy/plantations/material/BookOilPalm2.html

WWF. 2007. "Mesoamerican Reef: The Atlantic Ocean's Largest Coral Reef." Washington, DC: World Wildlife Fund. Accessed July 2012. www.worldwildlife.org/what/wherewework/mesoamericanreef/WWFBinaryitem11345.pdf

———. 2011. "FAQ in response to 'Conservation's Dirty Secrets'" August 23, 2011. Accessed June 2012. http://www.wwf.org.au/news_resources/archives/faq_in_response_to_conservation_dirty_secrets/#anchor26

INDEX

ABOUT THE AUTHOR

Tanya Kerssen is a researcher at Food First/Institute for Food and Development Policy, where she analyzes the root causes of hunger and works to amplify the voices of social movements fighting to transform the global food system. She writes and teaches on the political economy of food, agriculture and peasant resistance, with a focus on Latin America and Africa. She is deeply engaged in solidarity work in support of Honduran land and democracy movements in the aftermath of the 2009 coup.

ABOUT FOOD FIRST

The Institute for Food and Development Policy, also known as Food First, is a nonprofit research and education-for-action center dedicated to investigating and exposing the root causes of hunger in a world of plenty. Our 37 years of research have shown that hunger is caused by poverty and injustice—not scarcity. Resources and decision-making are in the hands of a privileged few, depriving the majority of land, markets, dignified work and healthy food.

Founded in 1975 by Frances Moore Lappé, author of the best-selling *Diet for a Small Planet,* and food policy analyst Dr. Joseph Collins, Food First has published over 60 books, including the seminal *Food First: Beyond the Myth of Scarcity.* Hailed by the New York Times as "one of the most established food think tanks in the country," Food First's groundbreaking work continues to shape local, national and international policies and debates about hunger and development. Learn more at www.foodfirst.org

Become a Member!
We invite you to join Food First. As a member you will receive a 20 percent discount on all Food First books. You will also receive our quarterly publications, newsletter and backgrounders, providing information for action on current food and land struggles in the United States and around the world. All contributions are tax-deductible. Please visit our website for details at www.foodfirst.org or contact us at foodfirst@foodfirst.org or (510) 654-4400.

ALSO FROM FOOD FIRST BOOKS

Available from www.foodfirst.org

UNFINISHED PUZZLE Cuban Agriculture: The Challenges, Lessons and Opportunities

By May Ling Chan and Eduardo Francisco Freyre

Cuba's support for small farmers and sustainable agriculture is unparalleled. Nonetheless, the country continues to import large amounts of food. This book explores the contradictions of the Cuban food system and what the future holds for its producers and consumers.

ISBN 978-0-935028-42-3

December 2012, $14.95

Food Movements Unite! Strategies to Transform Our Food System

Edited by Eric Holt-Giménez, Preface by Samir Amin

This book brings together the insights of farmers, workers and activists from rural and urban communities around the globe covering topics such as the global fight for climate justice; the Black Panther Party's food justice legacy; women's autonomy; and food sovereignty in Africa. Contributors to this volume address the critical question: "How can we unite to transform the global food system?"

ISBN: 978–0–935028–38–6

November 2011, $24.99, also available in Italian

Food Sovereignty: Reconnecting Food, Nature and Community

Edited by Annette Desmarais, Nettie Wiebe and Hannah Wittman

This book argues that food sovereignty is the means to achieving a system that will provide for the food needs of all people while respecting the principles of environmental sustainability, local empowerment and agrarian citizenship. Contributors include: Miguel Altieri, Walden Bello, Rachel Bezner Kerr, Jack Kloppenburg, Paul Nicholson and Raj Patel.

ISBN: 978-0-935028-37-9

November 2010, $24.95

Food Rebellions: Crisis and the Hunger for Justice
By Eric Holt-Giménez and Raj Patel with Annie Shattuck
Food Rebellions gives a detailed historical analysis of the events that led to the global food crisis of 2007/2008 and documents the grass-roots initiatives of social movements working to forge food sovereignty around the world.
ISBN: 978–0–935028–34–8
November 2009, $19.95

Agrofuels in the Americas
Edited by Rick Jonasse
Agrofuels in the Americas takes a critical look at the recent expansion of the agrofuels industry in the U.S. and Latin America and its effects on hunger, labor rights, trade and the environment.
ISBN: 978-0-935028-36-2
September 2009, $18.95

Beyond the Fence: A Journey to the Roots of the Migration Crisis
By Dori Stone
Beyond the Fence examines how US/Mexico policy affects families, farmers and businesses on both sides of the border, exposing irretrievable losses, but also hopeful advances.
ISBN: 978-0-935028-33-1
March 2009, $16.95

Alternatives to the Peace Corps: A Guide to Global Volunteer Opportunities (Twelfth Edition)
Edited by Caitlin Hachmyer
This easy-to-use guidebook is the original resource for finding community-based, grassroots volunteer work—the kind of work that changes the world, one person at a time.
ISBN: 978-0-935028-31-7
April 2008, $11.95

Promised Land: Competing Visions of Agrarian Reform
Edited by Peter Rosset, Raj Patel and Michael Courville
Agrarian reform is back at the center of the national and rural development debate. The essays in this volume critically analyze a wide range of competing visions of land reform.
ISBN: 978-0-935028-28-7
November 2006, $21.95

Campesino a Campesino: Voices from Latin America's Farmer to Farmer Movement for Sustainable Agriculture

By Eric Holt-Giménez

The voices and stories of dozens of farmers are captured in this history of the farmer-to-farmer movement in Central America, which describes the social, political, economic and environmental circumstances that shape this important movement.

ISBN: 978-0-935028-27-0

April 2006, $19.95

Basta! Land and the Zapatista Rebellion in Chiapas (Third Edition)

By George A. Collier with Elizabeth Lowery-Quaratiello

Foreword by Peter Rosset,

Now in its third and revised edition, this book paints a vivid picture of the Zapatista rebellion that shot into the international spotlight on January 1, 1994, in the impoverished state of Chiapas in southern Mexico.

ISBN: 0-935028-97-8

June 2005, $16.95

To Inherit the Earth: The Landless Movement and the Struggle for a New Brazil

By Angus Wright and Wendy Wolford

To Inherit the Earth tells the dramatic story of Brazil's Landless Workers' Movement, or MST, the millions of poor, landless, jobless men and women who, through their own nonviolent efforts, have secured rights to over 20 million acres of farmland.

ISBN: 978-0-935028-90-4

May 2003, $15.95

Food First books are available online at www.foodfirst.org or from your local independent bookseller. To find an independent bookseller in your area, visit www.booksense.com. You can also order directly from our distributor, Perseus Distribution, by calling (800) 343-4499.